Tackle Skating

By the same author

The Sense in Sport
This Skating Age
The Magic of Skiing
Winter Sports
Success in Ice Skating
International Encyclopaedia of Winter Sports
Let's Go Skating

Tackle Skating

Howard Bass

Stanley Paul, London

Stanley Paul & Co Limited
3 Fitzroy Square, London W 1 P 6JD

An imprint of the Hutchinson Publishing Group

London Melbourne Sydney Auckland
Wellington Johannesburg and agencies
throughout the world

First published 1978

Set in Monotype Times New Roman

Printed in Great Britain by litho at The Anchor Press Ltd
and bound by Wm Brendon & Son Ltd
both of Tiptree, Essex

British Library CIP data
Bass, Howard
  Tackle skating.
  1. Skating
  I. Title
  796.9'1   GV849

ISBN 0 09 133740 2 cased
      0 09 133741 0 paper

Contents

CONTENTS

Skating is an exercise fitted for both old and young. It may be taken as an exacting art or merely as a pleasant diversion; but for those who intend to practise for competitions, it has endless attractions. Its difficulties make it all the more interesting. There are always new fields to conquer. From the point of view of health, there are few if any exercises to compare with it; and it has the advantage of being equally fascinating when practised alone or in the delightful form of pair skating.

MADGE SYERS

Acknowledgements

All the photographs in this book except the one on page
79 (Sporting Pictures) were taken by Tony Duffy,
the award-winning specialist in international sports
photography.

The author acknowledges invaluable co-operation from
Gerald Powell of Carl Zeiss (Oberkochen) Ltd, Hugh
Riopelle of Air Canada, Ann Roberts of Inter-Continental
Hotels and Margaret Vernal

1 Introduction

Skating on ice is the most health-giving sport, invigorating whether indoors or out. It is good for the posture, recommended to strengthen weak ankles and other ailments of the limbs, an easy avenue to physical fitness and a simple recreation for all the family to enjoy within moments of starting. It is also a complex, absorbing art, with infinite scope for improvement which can happily fill all the hours one can spare in a lifetime.

The quotation preceding this chapter is no less apt today than when first penned in 1906 by Madge Syers, four years after that renowned British skater struck an early blow for women's lib as runner-up to Ulrich Salchow in the world figure skating championships, then open to men and women. A separate event for the so-called weaker sex was not instituted until 1906 and Mrs Syers comfortably gained the title in each of its first two seasons.

Although now divided into several sophisticated divisions – figure skating for men, women and pairs, ice dancing and men's and women's speed skating – modern ice skating evolved from the simplest beginnings. It is steeped far earlier in history than the origins of most competitive recreations. Properly organized championships also date back longer than the majority of today's other major sports.

Evolving, like skiing, from a primitive means of transport more than 3000 years ago, skating was originally performed on blades crudely made from animal bones, the steel skate dating from 1850.

The early history is recounted in greater detail in my book, *Let's Go Skating* (Stanley Paul, London; St Martins, New York). That work contains much general information complementary to this more specifically instructive volume.

In no sport is a coach more essential than in figure skating – for the serious competitor, that is. But for the less ambitious, purely recreative skater content with elementary progress, no professional tuition necessarily need be sought.

Let it be underlined at the outset that this author has been no expert performer, theoretical knowledge far outweighing practical ability. After learning to skate with minimal instruction on Swiss outdoor and British indoor rinks, more comprehensive technical understanding was subsequently acquired during three decades as a writer specializing in sports on ice and snow, gaining from many close associations with champions and instructors throughout the world.

The furtherance of international goodwill and mutual understanding through the medium of all sport has been a prime personal consideration throughout extensive global travel. An international viewpoint is thus intentionally dominant in this edition; as it is for English-speaking readers, it is mindful particularly of their interests. Having spent appreciable time in the United States and Canada, these nations and my native Britain are especially concerned, also the now rapidly expanding activities in later-developing skating nations.

The first properly maintained ice rink started in New York's Central Park in 1858. The same year, Canada's first covered rink was erected in Quebec City. Britain's first artificially frozen rink opened in 1876. The first British club was formed in Edinburgh in 1784, when of course only natural ice was available. The first North American club was founded in Philadelphia in 1849.

The sport's first national administration, the National

Skating Association of Great Britain, was founded in 1879, originally to administer speed skating and subsequently incorporating figure skating. The United States Amateur Skating Association was inaugurated in 1886 and that of the Canadians in 1887. Their present-day offshoots, the United States Figure Skating Association and the Canadian Figure Skating Association, date from 1921 and 1934 respectively.

The International Skating Union was instituted in 1892 and, now with thirty-two member nations, supervises both speed and figure skating, the latter including ice dancing. Officially recognized world speed skating championships began in 1893 and world figure skating championships in 1896. Figure skating became an Olympic sport in 1908, followed by speed skating in 1924.

The organizing pulses of competitive skating in Britain, Canada and the United States, the respective national association headquarters in London, Ottawa and Boston, and the International Skating Union offices in Davos, Switzerland – almost as English-speaking – are hives of administrative industry catering for countless thousands of enthusiasts in all grades.

When a fascinated guest of each of these nerve-centres, I have been impressed by the seemingly indefatigable back-room activity of hard-worked officials, whether paid or honorary. In each country, some part of their work through the years has been recorded for posterity in extensive libraries specializing in the sport. Perhaps the most comprehensive is, appropriately, at Davos, where George Häsler, the former I S U secretary, has built up a remarkable stock of books with painstaking devotion.

Leisure skating, for the sheer pleasure and social benefits of gliding around the rink without being particularly skilful, is in itself healthfully rewarding, exhilarating and inexpensive. To ascend the scale of competence, proficiency tests, graded from elementary to advanced ability, are the normal means of progress. Eligibility to enter competitions and championships at any level is based on holding a pass certificate in the requisite standard.

The higher one ascends in technical ability, the more time-consuming and costly this sport becomes, but it is possible eventually to cash in handsomely by turning professional, either to teach others or to perform in ice shows, perhaps thus touring the world while being paid to do what one enjoys.

All skaters aspiring to take any grade of proficiency test in figures, free skating, pair skating or ice dancing, or those with speed events in mind, should join their national association, which will supply members with all details of tests and competitions in the country concerned.

The addresses of national association secretaries in English-speaking countries affiliated to the International Skating Union are:

Australia

Figure skating: Wendy A. Langton, secretary, National Ice Skating Association of Australia, Flat 8, 56 Ramsgate Avenue, Bondi Beach, New South Wales, 2026.
Speed skating: Bob Roberts, secretary, Australian Amateur Ice Racing Council, 6 Loville Avenue, Peakhurst 2210, Sydney, New South Wales.

Canada

Figure skating: Douglas Gunter, executive manager, The Canadian Figure Skating Association, 333 River Road, Ottawa, Ontario K1L 8B9.

Speed skating: Marc Côté, executive director, Canadian Amateur Speed Skating Association, 333 River Road, Ottawa, Ontario K1L 8B9.

Great Britain

Figure and speed: A. R. Drake, secretary, National Skating Association of Great Britain, 117 Charterhouse Street, London, EC1M 6AT.

New Zealand

Figure and speed: Mrs Pamela B. Hewinson, secretary, New Zealand Ice Skating Association, 8b Peters Lane, Christchurch 2.

South Africa

Figure skating: Miss D. M. Simmonds, secretary, South African Ice Skating Association, 21 Callevera, 461 Windermere Road, Durban, Natal 4001.
Speed skating: Mrs Y. Bissett, secretary, South African Speed Skating Association, PO Box 1457, Benoni 1500, Transvaal.

United States of America

Figure Skating: William J. Brennan, Jr, secretary, United States Figure Skating Association, 129 East 69th Street, New York, NY 10021.
Speed Skating: Bill Cushman, secretary, United States International Speed Skating Association, 1166 Sherren Street West, St Paul, Minn. 55113.

The reader who has yet to visit an ice rink or whose present knowledge of skating is limited to what has been watched on the television or cinema screen will, it is hoped, share with the already experienced skater the practical guidance and general interest in the sport which this book aims to satisfy.

While helping anyone to learn the rudiments, if necessary without the aid of an instructor, it is reiterated that the more advanced technical explanations and hints are intended as a supplement, but never a substitute, for good coaching on the ice, without which no appreciable progress can be reasonably expected by the ambitious.

Happy skating, everyone.

2 The ice scene

Within recent decades, very many people who might well have taken up skating never did, simply because no rink existed within easy access of their home. This situation still applies today, though happily to a lesser extent.

Despite its long history, only in this century has skating seriously developed beyond a winter outdoor recreation dependent on temperatures below freezing point. The sport subsequently developed in a comfortable and congenial all-year-round indoor atmosphere only in proportion to the amount of mechanically frozen ice made available.

The best skaters of yesteryear were reared on natural outdoor ice, so it is no accident that Scandinavians were particularly prominent. Now, ironically, they are much less to the fore because they were later than most to build indoor rinks.

Speed skating is still woefully short of artificially frozen international 400-metre circuits, which require so much more space. There are only three major outdoor tracks in the United States today, at West Allis, Wisconsin; Keystone, Colorado; and the Olympic circuit at Lake Placid, in New York State. Many North American, British and European racers have been largely dependent on training facilities in Norway and Holland.

Popular though skating is, the sport is still very much in its infancy, so far as numbers of participants are concerned, but one can visualize the day when rinks will be as commonplace as public swimming pools with at least one civic rink in every sizable town.

High costs of erection and maintenance have fettered progress in this direction, but more economic methods are becoming available and, obviously, sport on skates will be tomorrow's in-recreation, not least ice hockey, which – as already in northern Europe and Canada – will become as generally popular as are team games on grass. In Finland, Sweden or Canada, more schoolboys in the streets are seen carrying ice hockey sticks than football boots, but this book will not enlarge on the game because it warrants its own more specialized volume.

Suffice to note that – with the potential interest in curling, ice hockey, speed skating, figure skating and ice dancing – given enough ice there is a very long way to go before there can be anything like sufficient rinks to satisfy tomorrow's demand.

It is quite remarkable to reflect that, only a couple of decades ago, world figure skating championships took place on outdoor rinks. Covered, electrically frozen surfaces have been obligatory only since 1967 and, although many of today's top figure skaters have never performed on natural ice, the generation before them certainly did. The change during their lifetime has been phenomenal.

At least two million ice skaters of varying grades now participate in Canada on some two thousand rinks. On a similar number of rinks, the sport is believed to attract well over that figure in the United States.

The Canadian Figure Skating Association, the largest organization of its kind in the world, has a membership fast approaching two hundred thousand in more than a thousand affiliated clubs – the more dedicated enthusiasts who represent only a small proportion of Canadians who skate.

16

The United States pair champions, Randy Gardner and Tia Babilonia, about to enter a death spiral (*above*) and (*below*) nearing the end of the movement. Note how Tia's hair brushes the ice during this daring spin.

The sport is expanding rapidly in nearly all of the thirty-two member nations of the International Skating Union, and these include countries, like Spain and South Africa, where skating is hardly possible without artificial refrigeration.

A recent national resurgence in Australia has been sparked by state and federal government grants which have enabled notable improvements at the main Sydney rink. International championships have yet to reach Australia and New Zealand, but South Africa, whose national ice skating association dates from 1931, now boasts a dozen indoor rinks, and has staged successful international tournaments in Johannesburg. In 1977, Japan hosted the first world figure skating championships to be held in Asia, stimulated by the success of the 1972 Olympic skating at Sapporo.

Thriving indoor rinks throughout Europe have been augmented by mechanically frozen surfaces even in Swiss and Austrian Alpine resorts, despite the availability of natural ice in such areas.

Progress in Britain was retarded by post-war economic difficulties which other European nations overcame more quickly. In Britain there are only thirty-eight rinks – twenty-two in England, fifteen in Scotland and one in Wales. This compares with more than a hundred rinks in France, of which fifteen are in the Paris area, as opposed to London's five. Holland has ten artificial outdoor ice speed circuits, yet Britain has none.

But the pressing demand for more ice in the United Kingdom is likely to lead eventually to many more rinks. Nearly every Scottish rink at present is dominated by curling. In England, conversely, the curlers hardly get a look in. Clearly, skating would expand fast in Scotland and curling would flourish in England, given more ice.

No international championships have been staged in

Britain since 1950 because the nation does not possess the requisite two suitable and reasonably close full-size rinks (one for practice, the other with adequate spectator accommodation). Eventually, a sprouting of new civic rinks is anticipated as newly researched developments enable appreciably lower costs.

There are two ways of enjoying rink facilities – by paying admission at public sessions, usually of three hours' duration, or by joining a club at the rink on a season-ticket basis. The latter style is particularly successful in the United States.

At almost every rink, skates and boots may be readily hired. At most, skate shops exist for the sale and servicing of skates and, in many cases, appropriate clothing and accessories may also be purchased.

National associations will gladly advise about the nearest facilities to one's home. In localities fortunate enough to have any, local education authorities probably include rink lessons in the school's recreational syllabus. If not, parents should press for such recognition on a par with other sports.

Equally, would-be skaters living in well-populated areas still without rinks are advised to agitate – and inspire others to join them – by pressing relevant local council departments or members of parliament on the grounds that, if you do not voice a grievance, nobody knows you have one. There is no doubt that pressure of numbers can stimulate action by sparking awareness of a need and demand.

There are several vital factors to be considered by anyone contemplating the building of a new ice rink. Vogues may change and future and existing needs may not be quite the same.

Many civic and private rink owners have built 'participation-only' rinks without thought for spectator provision originally not required. It is wise to take a long-term view and assume that, if not in the immediate future, a day can come when the rink would be more profitably served by alternative uses.

Rink managements often live to rue the fact that their ice area is not of suitable dimensions for ice hockey, curling, indoor speed skating or ice shows and that there is not room for sufficient spectators to make viable an event for which the rink was not at first intended.

The message here is clear, Whatever the original purpose, install an ice area of suitable size for any of the above activities and, if seats are not fitted in the first instance, at least allow adequate space, if reasonably possible, for housing upwards of five thousand spectators at a later date.

The ideal measurements of an all-purpose rink are not less than 60 metres (200 ft) long and 26 metres (85 ft) wide. 30 metres (100 ft) wide is better. Senior figure skating championships, league ice hockey games or indoor speed skating matches can all be staged perfectly and profitably, if well promoted, on ice measuring 60 by 30 metres (200 by 100 ft), the area recommended by the I S U.

3 What to wear

Skates, boots and skate-guards are the only essential special equipment required, skate-guards being vital to the protection of the skate blades when walking on the skates while off the ice.

The beginner is advised to hire a skating set (boots with skates attached) for the first few sessions, but only until deciding to pursue the sport indefinitely. Opt for a snug-fitting full size or half-size smaller than street shoes if reasonably comfortable.

As with swimming or riding, one soon either instinctively takes to the sport or rejects it as 'not for me', but, in the event of any initial doubt, it must be remembered that initial tolerance is necessary to overcome the inevitable spills and indignities which everyone at first has to endure. Also, hired equipment is bound to be less comfortable than one's own.

Just as a novice swimmer has breathing and floating problems and a new rider acquires a sore seat, so a skating tyro will experience early discomfort well worth enduring.

The majority emerge happily triumphant, to discover a whole new area of enjoyment, but the few who stumble by the wayside will have wasted money spent on new equipment before experimenting with rented skates and boots.

So, assuming one has come through the 'initiation test' with undiminished ardour, hired equipment should be forgotten and the immediate concern becomes the purchase of suitable skates and boots. A set already fixed together is not recommended. Better to select the most appropriate blades and the best-fitting boots and then have them screwed together. Most ice rink shops are ideally suited for all this because the shop assistants are usually technical experts in this specialized field.

So first choose the right boots. Although often called shoes, boots are really the better description because they cover the ankles. Adults are advised to buy as good quality as can be afforded. For children soon likely to grow out of them, a cheaper pair may be prudent so long as the fit is comfortable and not too tight.

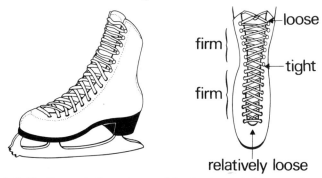

Left: The figure skating set, comprising boot and skate screwed together. *Right:* A correctly laced boot. Leave the lowest pair of eyelets relatively loose so that the toes are not cramped, then tie more firmly until reaching the ankle area, which should be tied tightly, particularly round the top pair of eyelets, above which most boots are equipped with five or six pairs of hooks. The bottom pair of hooks should be tightly tied and the rest firmly except the top pair of hooks. These should be loose enough to enable a finger to be inserted between sock and boot (to ease circulation)

Before even trying any on, make sure that the boots are of top-grain leather, with linings of leather and not canvas. They should have strong ankle supports, to prevent the feet from slipping to the sides, and be reinforced with inner arches. The soles must be rigid enough to retain the screws which hold the metal mounts of the skate blades.

The fit is of paramount importance, at least half a size smaller than normal footwear, fitting tightly at heel, ankle and instep, but more loosely round the toes. When fitting, thin woollen socks or stockings should be worn because the boot must come to feel part of the foot and this it cannot do if too thick a sock or stocking is worn.

Thick hose can restrict proper circulation and be surprisingly less warm than a thinner garment. If a new boot is fitted over silk or nylon stockings or tights, it can comfortably take an ankle sock or woollen stocking later.

Next, the skates. Newcomers and all purely recreational skaters should choose the 'figure' skate, readily distinguishable from the 'hockey' or 'speed' skate by the 'teeth' at the front end of the blade. These teeth are known as a toe-rake or toe-pick, of particular importance for spinning and jumping, which will not concern the beginner.

The skate blade should be of high-tempered steel, nickel or chrome plated. The best-known make, sold throughout the world, is M K, with a wide range catering for every grade of performer (special blades for speed skating are described in a later chapter).

A magnified impression of a skate blade's edge touching the ice. The arch emphasizes the hollow grind between the two edges

The figure blade is slightly curved from toe to heel, set on a two-metre (seven-foot) radius. Fractionally longer than the length of the boot, the blade is approximately 3 mm

($\frac{1}{8}$ in.) wide. Its underneath, on which one skates, is not flat but has a hollow concave ridge along its length. This is termed 'hollow-ground'.

Each side of the ridge is called an 'edge'. The edge nearer the inside of the foot is the inside edge, the other the outside edge. All technical movements in figure skating are performed on one of these edges so that, whether in forward or backward motion, the skate is not flat but always moving at an angle to the ice.

There are skates designed for beginners, moderate and advanced performers. Some models are better for figures and others for free skating, so when a performer graduates to competition level it is recommended that a set of each kind be acquired. An elementary model for figures, such as the Rinkmaster or Single Star, is ideal for a first all-purpose pair.

The skates are normally marked to correspond with the boot size. To double-check, the distance between the front and rear extremities of the mounting plates which screw to the boot should be about 4·5 mm ($\frac{1}{5}$ in.) shorter than the length of the boot.

The really serious skater will be happier with two pairs if the pocket allows so that one is always available if and as repair becomes necessary; it will also eliminate inconvenience while a pair is being re-ground, quite apart from the dilemma confronting anyone unlucky enough to lose a pair.

The blades need to be re-ground from time to time, according to wear, to retain a sharpness of edges conducive to maintaining the proper easy-gliding action.

When the right boots and skates have been duly selected and purchased, it is best to have each skate screwed to the boot so that the blade is slightly nearer the inside of the foot rather than precisely down the centre of the sole and heel.

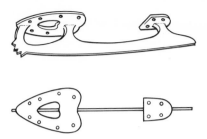

These two views of a figure skate, from side-on and from above, show the screw-holes used for fitting to the sole of the boot

Most skaters find that the blade fits ideally underneath a point between the big toe and second toe, getting the body weight more naturally over the skate than dead along the centre of the sole. A good rink skate-shop fitter will co-operate by screwing the skates to the boots temporarily (not using every screw), so that they may be tried in more than one alternative position before deciding which seems most suitable and finally fixing them together more thoroughly.

The other essential part of equipment is a pair of rubber or plastic skate-guards, which fit neatly over the blades to enable walking in reasonable comfort between the ice and changing-room. Regular skaters can be seen taking off their guards just before going on to the ice and putting them on again immediately after coming off. This prevents the sharp edges from being blunted, as they certainly would be if one walked many steps on wood or concrete.

Skate-guards should also protect the skates when carried to and from the rink, even if in a bag, but should not be fitted over blades before removing any slush. The skate-guards can be taken off at home and care should be taken to keep the blades dry from condensation. When left for any appreciable length of time, a little oil smeared on the skates will help prolong their active life.

The skate blades should be sharpened after about a dozen skating sessions or an estimated thirty hours' use, but the rink-shop expert who sharpens them should be consulted when in doubt because it is equally important not to have them ground too often as too seldom. It is a skilled job and any experienced skater will confirm the wisdom of finding a tried and trusted skate-grinder.

Boots will retain better shape and be more comfortable if fitted with trees or tightly stuffed with paper before being put away. Boots can be best kept in good order by using a quality non-spirit cleaner which will not damage or dry out the leather. This also is obtainable at all good rink skate-shops. Reliable old footwear is cherished because it becomes so well moulded to the shape of the feet, so offset any possibility of rotting with an occasional coat of heel and sole enamel to prevent moisture from separating the heel and outer sole layers.

Care must be taken not to dry a skating set too near a fire or radiator because the contrasting extremes of temperature could possibly crack the blades, damage the boot leather or even adversely affect glue in the boots.

Before leaving the subject of boots, a word about lacing should not come amiss because it is a little art in itself. First make sure the laces are loose all the way down before putting on the boot, then see that the heel is well back in the boot and pull up the tongue firmly.

To minimize any possible loosening of hooks and eyelets, do not tug too sharply when lacing up, nor bend down and pull upwards, but raise each foot in turn to waist level and pull the laces towards the body rather than upwards.

When tying laces, leave the bottom area loose so that the toes are not cramped. Once past the lowest pair of eyelets, tie the laces firmly until reaching the ankle area. Around the ankles they should be much tighter. This area

Holding a hand below the free knee adds a variation to this elegant
forward spiral by Anett Poetzsch, of East Germany, who became
world champion in 1978.

on most boots coincides with the top pair of eyelets, from which point upwards hooks usually begin. The lowest hooks should be tightly tied, the next a little less firmly, but the highest hooks must be tied more loosely so that it is easily possible to insert a finger between sock and boot. Boots tied too tightly at the top can restrict circulation.

On or off the ice, one should never move about with footwear unlaced. Without the support of properly fastened boots, ankle injuries can result and there is also the risk of a blade cutting, or the wearer tripping over, a dangling lace.

Thus, the final knot is especially important. A one-and-a-half bow is better-looking and more reliable than a double bow. First tie a loose single bow, then put the left-hand loop through under the loose knot and pull tight. This can be easily untied like a single bow. The loose ends may be tidily tucked beside the tongue.

While stressing the wisdom of buying good-quality boots and skates, it is compensating to note that no other special equipment or clothing need be purchased for recreational skating.

For indoor rinks, dependent on what heating there may be, normal sports trousers with shirt and sweater are quite suitable for men and boys. A slightly full skirt or slacks with jumper are ideal for women and girls.

For everyone, light woollen socks are recommended. Woollen gloves not only keep the hands warm, but afford sensible protection: most injuries from skating accidents consist of minor cuts or bruises on the hands. Headgear, if any, should be close-fitting, but long hair should not be tethered by hairpins, which can be dangerous if they fall on the ice.

Experienced male skaters may graduate to tighter-fitting trousers. Close-fitting, neatly cut jackets with matching tights and perhaps a badge on the breast pocket would be the height of fashion.

More sophisticated female attire can include suntan-coloured tights and pants toning with skating skirt over the tights. Skirts may be worn very short, so that when the skater is standing upright the hem just hides the pants.

Except when conditions are warm enough for the bare legs, which no doubt feel and look fine for the fair sex, silk, nylon or woollen tights or stockings will keep the muscles warm and reduce the chances of rheumatic tendencies in later life. Light ankle socks should always be worn, with or without tights or stockings.

In poorly heated indoor rinks or when skating outdoors, obviously warmer wear is necessary, with emphasis on heavier woollens. When skating at winter resorts, the snow-reflected sunshine makes protective cream and sun spectacles a must.

Those who skate much in such conditions are recommended to wear the newly perfected Umbramatic lenses which are almost clear in dull light, but, within minutes of moving into sunshine, darken automatically to sunglass density. Then, when back in the shade, they become clear again. They are equally ideal for summer beachwear.

The makers, Zeiss, also market a new Sunscene Safety spectacle frame, a further improvement with an adjustable and detachable headband fitted to the side wires which gives added security during active sports. Wearers thus eliminate any fear of their spectacles falling on to the ice. I wear prescription Umbramatic lenses in Sunscene Safety frames on all winter sports and summer outdoor activities because it outdates the previous need to interchange between ordinary clear prescription lenses and sunglasses or mess about with clip-ons. Incidentally, the same tone-changing qualities are available for sunglasses not needing prescription; these are called Umbrals.

For the advanced skater, suitable attire for competitions and championships is a separate consideration, involving comfort, practicability and a prudent element of showmanship. This is where 'keeping up with the Joneses' can easily hit the pocket, though simple, inexpensive apparel can often prove sufficiently effective.

Championship judges may not award any marks for what the skater wears, but they do mark for artistic presentation, so smartness of appearance can help more than hinder in this direction. In any case, a competitor naturally wants to look attractively dressed when appearing before the public.

Well-tailored, close-fitting one-piece suits are frequently worn by men in the championship class, in colours usually matching their partners if in pair or ice dance events.

Women competitors find crêpe and other elastic materials have the advantage of retaining shape and allowing maximum freedom of movement. Chiffon and lamé also are well favoured. Elaborate decorative trimmings of sequins or rhinestones are not quite so fashionable as they used to be, simplicity often proving more effective than too much fussiness of detail.

The latter tends to emphasize the plumper figure, as do shiny materials like lamé or satin. It is perhaps better to concentrate on a cut of the costume which shows off the figure to best effect rather than on subtle detail of embroidery which cannot be appreciated at a distance.

Black or white, or anything particularly dazzling, may not be ideal for television. However magnificent the dress, all will be spoilt by soiled boots and this applies especially if they are meant to be white. Make sure that they really are newly cleaned for the big event.

4   The first steps

The great, never-to-be-forgotten day has come. Courage has been taken in both feet, skates and boots have been put on and properly laced up. A new dimension of movement is to be experienced, but initial progress will be slow and tedious, so patience and determination are required. It will all prove well worthwhile.

Assuming a hired skating set is being worn, allowance must be made for the near-certainty that the fit will not be anything like so comfortable as one's own – soon to be selected and fitted – probably after this and a couple more sessions at the rink.

For the next hour or more, the complete beginner is going to feel decidedly awkward and embarrassed. It is an ordeal which each champion has had to endure on this momentous day of ice baptism. But it is a memorable adventure into the great unknown. Some falls are inevitable but harmless. By the time one has learned to stand up, one may not feel eager to sit, but a few tender contusions are a small price to pay for the years of enjoyment to follow.

This will be the worst day. The next should be much easier and excitement will mount afterwards as progress follows relatively fast when the thrilling new movements and sense of balance are experienced, together with the sudden realization that those first sessions were indeed paying handsome dividends for the trouble and perseverance taken, however dubious or even discouraged one at first might have felt.

It has been suggested already that an instructor is not essential for an unambitious recreational skater, but obviously a tutor at any time can help accelerate progress and the cost of a twenty-minute or half-hour session with a junior coach at the very first rink visit could prove a sound investment.

Assistance at this time would help confidence and sense of balance to develop more quickly, making a second visit much easier without such help. Alternatively, the friendly hand of another skater may be sought. Usually, there is someone willing, whose own first outing is still a vivid memory. This is how new friendships are quickly won on the ice rink. From the outset, remember that skating is basically a gliding action on one skate at a time, the blade moving according to the degree of body weight above it.

The ice will seem more slippery during the first half-hour than it ever will again, because soon the control of weight and balance will instinctively counteract that first uneasiness.

First, feel the ice with very short forward gliding movements without lifting either skate from the ice and be conscious of inclining the weight rather more on the inside edge of the blade. Hold the rink barrier with one hand during these tentative steps. With or without someone else's guidance, it should soon be possible to stay safely upright without relying on the barrier so often. Then is the time to try skating forwards properly.

First forward steps

Stand with feet parallel and about 30 cm (12 in.) apart, with knees slightly bent and arms held outwards and slightly forwards, with hands at about hip level. Then, for the first stroke, swivel the left foot out to an angle of 45 degrees, at the same time consciously inclining the left ankle sufficiently inwards to feel the inside edge of the left blade contacting the ice.

With weight over the left foot and knees slightly bent, the left foot gives impetus to help the first forward movement with the right when leaning forward on to the right foot, transferring the weight over it. With the ankle kept as upright as possible, a forward gliding movement will be experienced on the right skate, with emphasis now on the blade's outside edge.

Maintaining an erect posture as the right foot glides forward, lift the left foot very fractionally clear of the ice and move it gently up alongside the right. Then, for the second stroke, turn the right foot out to an angle of 45 degrees, inclining the right ankle enough to feel the inside edge, and push on to the left foot, transferring the weight over it while mindful that the left shoulder should be well to the left.

Thus alternate gliding strokes are taken without lifting the disengaged foot higher than absolutely necessary during the early learning stages. The body should be kept as upright as possible, with the eyes focussed ahead and not at the feet. Each striding stroke can be gradually lengthened as confidence and ability grows.

Each forward stroke should be weighted over the whole skate, never on the front or toe of the blade. It will be progressively easier to feel the outside edge of the skating blade, as distinct from the flat, and to feel the left shoulder leaning further to the left when moving forward on the left skate, and vice versa with the right. So, a confident sense of balance develops comparable to that acquired when learning to ride a bicycle.

It will become quickly apparent that the forward left-foot stroke takes one in a slight curve to the left, and vice versa with the right; one does not, in fact, skate in a straight line but veers alternately from one side to the other. Remember to bend the knees well at the start of each stroke and to hold the arms about waist high, with palms downwards.

Learn to relax during the inevitable fall before acquiring a more instinctive sense of balance. One must avoid grabbing wildly at another skater. Do not scramble to get up, but kneel first on one knee, push on to the ice with both hands and, with skates close together in V-formation, rise carefully.

Braking

In fairness to one's self and everyone else on the rink, it is a beginner's duty to learn how to stop safely as soon as elementary forward skating has been accomplished. Once able to skate around the rink forwards, enthusiasm mounts and it becomes very tempting to increase speed and even to learn skating backwards, as I did – before thinking about how to stop effectively in emergency, to avoid hitting a prone body suddenly in one's path, for instance.

The most elementary means of braking for beginners when skating forwards is by dragging the inner side of the non-skating blade lightly on the ice behind the skating foot, at the same time maintaining body weight forward over the skating foot. As the disengaged blade touches the ice, snowy flakes gather in front of it, assisting the slowing-down, and one finishes with the feet in a T-formation, the heel of the front foot just in front of, and almost touching, the inside middle of the skating foot.

Another simple method of braking is to put the heel of the disengaged skate on the ice in front of the skating foot. In either case, do it gently without jerking.

A further elementary way of stopping can be achieved by adopting the 'snowplough' movement familiar to skiers.

34

Three methods of braking. Positions of feet in (*left to right*) the 'T' stop, the snow-plough and the more advanced skid stop

Put the non-skating foot on to the ice so that both feet are gliding forwards and parallel, with knees slightly bent and arms outwards and slightly forward at waist level. Force both heels outwards to form a V-formation, at the same time taking care to keep a reasonable gap of at least 15 cm (6 in.) between the toes. The braking is made more efficient when concluding this movement by bending the knees still further and inclining the blades more on to their inner edges.

The beginner is advised *not* to attempt the more advanced 'skid' or 'hockey' stop until a greater degree of all-round skating competence has been attained. This more difficult stop is achieved by gliding on both skates and quarter-turning both feet sideways to skid, with the weight pressed against the sides of the skates. The action is best accomplished by first straightening the knees and then bending them at the moment of halting, at the same time counter-rotating the waist. It is not easy and takes much practice to perfect, but, when performed correctly, can look quite spectacular.

First backward steps

When learning to drive a motor car, my instructor from the outset encouraged me to move forward from a stationary position without touching the accelerator. This quickly taught me how to feel the 'sensitivity' position of the clutch and earlier control was thus achieved.

By the same token, one can skate forwards or backwards very slowly, starting from a stationary position, without lifting either foot off the ice and this single exercise conveys in a practical way an early idea of how weight transference of the body influences movement of each skate without consciously trying by any other means to move either foot. Thus, another early sense of control is acquired – and this technique is of particular value during the initial phases of learning to skate backwards.

Having spent some half-a-dozen sessions improving the ability to skate forwards, the natural impulse is to want to learn a variation – and skating backwards is the obvious next addition to the repertoire.

First, stand with toes pointed in and heels out. Next, bending the knees, push from the inside of the left blade on to the right foot and raise the left leg just clear of the ice, travelling backwards on bent knee and slowly straightening it as the disengaged leg is brought alongside the right foot.

Strike off each step slowly, and bring the feet together again before making each new stroke. Try the movement first without attempting to lift either foot from the ice – just to give an earlier feel of how the body weight alone can cause motion.

It is important not to lean forwards when skating backwards. The head, shoulder and hip should be kept over the ball of the skating foot. The knees must not remain straight, but must bend readily with each gliding stroke backwards, then straighten gradually as the trailing foot is brought alongside the other, before again bending the knees to start the next backward stroke.

The weight of the body must not be taken off the foot which is doing the skating. Where the weight is, the action happens and, the more this fact is borne in mind, the easier it becomes to feel the correct positioning of body weight. It is this which is causing the feet to move in the direction intended.

Skating backwards, as might be logically supposed, corresponds to skating forwards with all the movements reversed. In other words, one still skates backwards on the outside edge, pushing from the inside edge, shifting weight over the stroking skate and gliding on a bent knee with posture erect.

A style feature to note is to avoid turning up the non-skating foot. The more it is pointed, the more elegant the movements become. When skating forwards, it is not normal to look behind to see where one has been. Correspondingly, when skating backwards, look over the shoulder in the direction one intends going – and do not look down at the feet.

Braking backwards

There are two fundamentals to remember when braking during a backward movement. The first is to keep the body well inclined forwards – that is, to the *rear* of the direction being skated. This is essential, to offset the risk of falling backwards in the direction being skated.

The second fundamental is the role played by the toe-picks. A very slight lifting of the heel while leaning well forward, away from the direction of skating, will give that feeling of 'clutch sensitivity'. Practice will determine the extent to which the heel is raised in relation to the speed of skating. Be sure to achieve the right action on each foot, one at a time, before attempting the exercise on both feet

37

simultaneously. Arms should be raised outwards, with hands about waist high, palms downward.

Forward crossovers

It is relatively easy for the beginner to skate forwards or backwards from one end of the rink to the other. To negotiate the corners properly requires another variation, known as the crossover, in which one foot is crossed over the other to enable easy continuation in a curve. The crossover action comes more easily after gathering momentum, but, to understand the technique, initially go through the movement from a stationary position.

A counter-clockwise crossover to the left comes more naturally to the right-hander. First, stand in a T-position, with left foot leading and right heel against the instep of the left foot. Left arm and shoulder back, right arm and shoulder forward. Bend the knees and push strongly with a forward stroke on the outside edge of the left skate, trailing a straightened right leg behind.

Now bring the right foot forward close past the left and cross it wide ahead and over on to the inside edge of the blade. As the right skate touches the ice, the feet should be parallel, with all weight transferring to the right leg at the moment of contact. This slick change of weight enables the left skate to glide off the ice, with the left leg extended and straight.

While the left leg is still in a crossed-under position, the glide should be consciously held for a few counts before bringing round the left skate close behind the right, ready for pushing into another forward stroke.

As when learning all skating actions, gradually work up more speed and a more accentuated lean. The crossover is a very natural movement, but early attention to correct positioning and timing of weight transference will make progress more rapid and agreeable.

The body must always lean towards the centre of the circle, i.e. towards the left when veering to the left. The

The cross-over is the natural way to corner when skating. For the counter-clockwise forward cross-over to the left, the easier direction for the right-handed skater, first lean well to the left while stroking on the outside edge of the left skate. Bend the right knee, passing the right skate over and well in front of the left skate to touch the ice on the other side of it, on the inside edge, so that both feet are skating parallel. The weight transfers completely on to the new skating foot, enabling the left to lift unhurriedly out from underneath the cross-over. Glide rather than push, when crossing over. Repeat the movement in circular direction with steady rhythm, gradually increasing speed and degree of lean. While cornering in a cross-over (forwards or backwards), the inside arm and shoulder should be lower and pressed back while the outside arm and shoulder are held higher and ahead

left shoulder is thus lower than the right throughout the movement. Each stroke is made on a bent knee, but the free knee should remain straight. The skater likening himself to an aeroplane banking or a bicycle turning will get the right sense of lean and keep the hip above the skating leg well in. A protruding hip is a common early error to correct before it can develop into a bad habit.

Corner-cutting crossovers not only widen one's versatility of movement. They strengthen the ability to use edges well and so are a fine preparation for proper figure skating.

Backward crossovers

The backward crossover is basically a case of reversing the forward version. For a clockwise direction, first take a long stroke on the left outside edge, with free leg well extended in front. The right leg should then be drawn back and well over in front of the left on to a strong inside backward edge. The timing of a neat shift of weight transference is the essence, leaving the left foot free of the ice, crossed under and extended outwards, with toe pointed.

The free foot is then brought round behind the right skate, ready for the next stroke. Push the stroke, glide the crossover, and look always in the direction of skating. The inside arm and shoulder should always be lower and pressed back; the outside arm and shoulder higher and more forward.

Forward and backward skating, braking, and clockwise and anti-clockwise crossovers cannot be practised too much. To get the right rhythmical timing, it can help at first to hum to oneself *The Skaters* waltz or music of similar tempo.

The ability to do all explained so far is in itself sufficient to derive much pleasure during rink recreational sessions. Many will be satisfied just to improve their standard of performance within this limited repertoire. Others will treat

In the backward cross-over the movements of the forward
cross-over are reversed. Stroke on a left back outside edge, with
free leg at first well extended in front, then to be drawn over
well in front and on to a strong inside back edge. A quick weight
transference at the moment of touching the right blade on the
ice enables the left crossed-under foot to be brought smoothly
around behind the right skate. The feet almost brush prior to the
next stroke. Push the stroke, but glide the cross-over.
Throughout, the head looks continually backward to the inside
of the curve being skated

it as merely the basic foundation on which to build a far
more varied and advanced skating capability. In the latter
case, rather than hurry to the next stage, plenty of practice
in the fundamental technique so far recounted, progressively lengthening the strokes and deepening the edges, is
strongly advised before graduating to real figure skating.

5 Figuring it out

Elementary ability to skate forwards and backwards will have made any newcomer aware that almost every skating movement is made on an edge and not on the flat of the blade. Not every beginner wishes to persevere with figures, though this is the next logical step for anyone with serious ambitions to become a proficient skater.

School figures, as they are called, are exercises which have been specially designed to provide the best technical groundwork for good skating, and learning to skate at least the more basic figures will provide the soundest preparation for the budding free skater or ice dancer.

Many people go to a school of ballroom dancing with the initial idea to learn just enough to be able to get round the floor sufficiently well for social enjoyment without trying to become very expert. The ballroom-dance tutor will probably try to encourage anyone revealing potential talent to train for graduated tests with certificates and medals in mind. It is for the learner to decide whether to pursue it that seriously or be content merely to dance well enough to get by for the occasional special function.

The situation is rather similar in skating. It can be absorbing to prepare for proficiency tests in figures, free skating, ice dancing or speed skating – the best way to progress – or one may be satisfied to stay a moderate performer, a decision perhaps dependent on time available and degree of ambition. There is also the possibility to pass tests and still make some kind of skating grade, albeit without solid technical foundation.

Whatever the choice, it must be stressed that learning at least the simplest figures is the best way from the outset to acquire good style and intelligent control of edges. To go straight on to free skating and ice dancing without practising any figures at all increases the chances of unconsciously cultivating early faults which, if unrealized and therefore neglected, can become progressively more difficult to eradicate and so retard the rate of satisfactory advance.

Every skating figure is based on only four moves on either foot – forward or backward on an outside edge and forward or backward on an inside edge. Skating on an edge entails a leaning of the body over that edge sufficient to cause a forward or backward movement in a curve – a curve which, if continued, would describe a circle.

As when the cyclist turns, the lean of a skater is proportionately greater according to the speed and angle of the curve. Just as a rider leans over with his cycle, so a skater must lean over *with* the edge of the blade being used. In either case, smoothness without jerking produces the best result.

Practise skating consciously on inside edges and on outside edges. Lengthen strokes as confidence grows, leaning farther over and forward while keeping the body weight over the skating foot. Bend the skating knee freely. Keep the non-skating foot pointed as elegantly as possible. Hold the arms about waist high for comfortable balance and good style, with palms downward. Hold the arms steadily, without waving them to and fro as when walking. Keep each skating stroke smooth, deliberate and unhurried, without jerking. The rinkside loudspeaker music will assist rhythmical timing. It feels good, it looks good and, by golly, as the beer advertisement says, it does you good. So good that having a go at figures may feel like a welcome challenge.

A school or compulsory figure (the word 'compulsory' meaning one required to be skated in a test or competition) consists of a two-lobe or three-lobe 'eight'. Each figure is skated three times, each tracing an indentation on the ice, the second and third efforts being superimposed as nearly as possible over the first – except, of course, where correction is needed.

Two sins to be avoided at all costs are skating on the 'flat' of the blade instead of on an edge, and 'double tracking', i.e. allowing the non-skating blade to touch the ice.

There are forty-one internationally recognized figures. Twenty-eight can be skated clockwise or anti-clockwise, which means a total of sixty-nine variations. Each is started from a stationary 'rest' position.

To avoid lapsing into a fault which only an expert might spot and eliminate before it becomes habit-forming, it is best to begin learning each new figure under the eye of a qualified instructor, whose fees for this would be well justified. After first being shown how to do a figure, it can be repeatedly practised, preferably with a friendly and more experienced skater watching.

Without attempting the mammoth task of taking each individual figure in meticulous detail (the rink instructor is much more suitable for that), it is hoped that the general comments which follow can serve to remind every figure aspirant of the correct approach and some pitfalls to avoid.

The technical merits of the tracing are not, as some might suppose, the sole criterion by which the figure is assessed. The tracing remaining for examination on the ice is one thing, the *modus operandi* another; the skater's control, position and balance are all taken into account. The positions of hands, fingers and non-skating foot are all critically assessed, as is the maintenance of a smooth, steady speed without jerking and the execution of changes from one foot to the other by means of a single stroke from the skate-edge and not from the toe.

Posture, then, is important. The head should be held as upright as possible, with eyes generally focussed between two and three feet ahead of the skating foot. The body from the waist up must be kept as erect as possible, yet suitably flexed for rotation as required. The skating leg should be bent at the start of each figure, straightening gradually without stiffening. The free leg should be very slightly bent and allowed to swing freely from the hip, with toe pointed in downward and outward direction.

The arms should be held outwards at around hip level (never higher than the waist), with the forward hand palm downwards, but with the rear hand palm more inclined at an angle automatically correct if the thumb is pointed upwards. Both arms move horizontally (except in backward changes, when the arm moves lower). Fingers are kept straight and together, without fanning.

Generally speaking, the diameter of each circle in the figure should be approximately three times the skater's height – a little smaller if the ice appears extra soft and therefore slow.

The outside forward eight is not only the first and best-known figure. It is also one of the most delightful to behold when done well and an instructor can usually assess any skater's real ability by the way this figure is performed. Every wobble, every deviation from a good circle is a degree short of perfection.

The ability to maintain a true and steady curve is very dependent on a correct start from 'rest', a strong but controlled push-off from the very centre of the eight to be skated. An imaginary line drawn through the centres of both circles is called the long axis (overall length) of a figure; the short axis is the width.

As a guiding example, when starting the outside forward eight on the right foot, stand in T-position, left instep to right heel, with right foot along the short axis and left foot parallel to the long axis. Before starting, a steady glance on each side along the long axis will enable planning a mental picture of both circles to be skated.

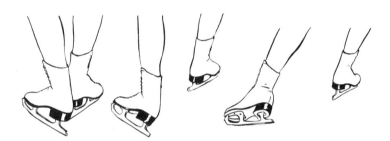

The first real figure-skating stroke. Push from standstill with feet in T-position, heel of right foot near left instep. Note left ankle turned in to anchor the skate to give thrust as the right skate goes forward. Then, when the body weight is fully over the right skating leg, the left foot lifts to become the free (non-skating) foot

With size of figure now firmly in mind, ensure standing with all weight on the left leg and with the left ankle turned in. Bend both knees when pushing away strongly from the left skate with a powerful thrust against the ice. As the weight transfers to the right leg, the left blade rises over the print (tracing).

With toe pointed, the non-skating left leg is kept straight and turned out from the hip, with the inside of the knee nearer to the ice. The free leg is held steadily in this position for the first semi-circle.

At this point the skating foot should be parallel with the shoulder line. Even though the weight should be still firmly over the skating foot, any lowering of the shoulder over the skating foot at this moment would throw the skater forward off balance.

The skating knee, still well bent since the push-off, now gradually begins to straighten as the free foot and leg pass forward and the arms and shoulders change, a re-positioning completed by the three-quarters circle, from where one glides without wavering.

With the shoulder over the skating foot now lower, the weight should be maintained throughout slightly to the rear of the centre of the blade's edge. To do this, it is necessary to lean slightly backward as the free leg moves forward. The entire movement must be smooth and unhurried. To sense the correct amount of lean, the free foot can actually brush the skating foot lightly as it passes and the arms also can brush the body.

Throughout the move, the hips must not rotate in the direction of the circle. To ensure this, the hip of the free leg must be pressed back as the foot moves forward. The free foot must not cross inside the circle. Mastering proper control of the hips will result in better balance and style.

As the circle nears completion, the free foot should be brought back beside the skating foot as both knees bend prior to the second push-off. As the skate reaches the original push-off mark, it should be turned sideways a full ninety degrees.

A firm, instant start at the second circle from the back of the right skate on to the left outside edge should ideally touch the ice over the original start-line. The pushing foot must turn fully sideways to enable the full body change. Maintaining similar speed to the first circle, all movements for the second are accordingly transposed.

47

The foregoing comments are intended solely as a 're-fresher' summary of points to bear in mind and not as a precise description of how to perform the eight. The latter one first learns much more readily from a rink or club instructor because it is really too difficult for most to comprehend originally from the written word.

Immense satisfaction can be derived from the ability to perform a figure eight on ice. It puts one immediately into a category above the average rink public-session skater and certainly whets the appetite to pursue this fascinating sport more avidly.

The abbreviations used to describe the following forty-one internationally recognized figures are normal skating terminology which, though at first bewildering, after a while becomes the easiest way to remember the movements:

R = right	b = backwards	T = three	RK = rocker
L = left	o = outside	LP = loop	C = counter
f = forwards	i = inside	B = bracket	

The higher the factor of a figure, the greater is its degree of difficulty. Thus, the simplest figures are more suited to elementary tests and competitions and the hardest ones are more commonly used in advanced tests and senior championships.

International ice figures

Figure	No. and description	Factor

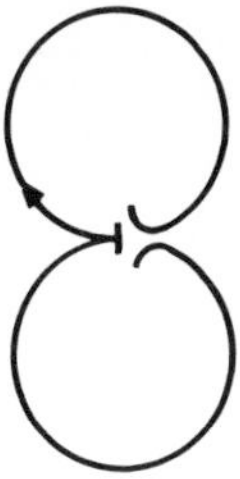

1

Curve eight

1. Rfo–Lfo	1
2. Rfi–Lfi	1
3. Rbo–Lbo	2
4. Rbi–Lbi	2

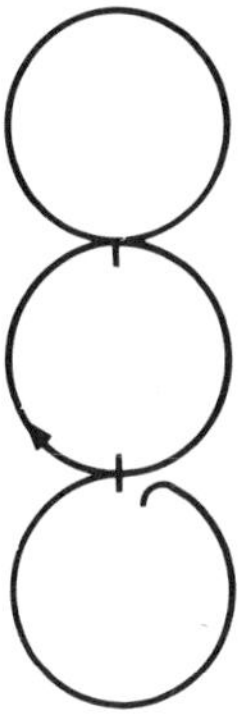

5a

Change

5a. Rfoi–Lfio	1
b. Lfoi–Rfio	1
6a. Rboi–Lbio	3
b. Lboi–Rbio	3

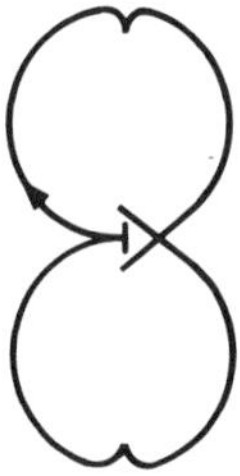

7

Three

7. RfoTbi–LfoTbi	2
8a. RfoTbi–LbiTfo	2
b. LfoTbi–RbiTfo	2
9a. RfiTbo–LboTfi	2
b. LfiTbo–RboTfl	2

49

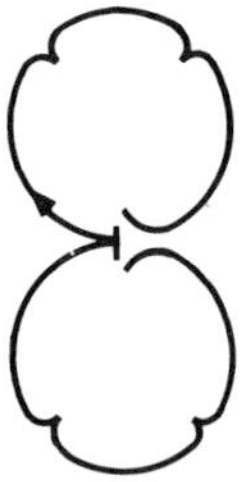

10

Double three

10.	RfoTbiTfo–LfoTbiTfo	2
11.	RfiTboTfi–LfiTboTfi	2
12.	RboTfiTbo–LboTfiTbo	3
13.	RbiTfoTbi–LbiTfoTbi	3

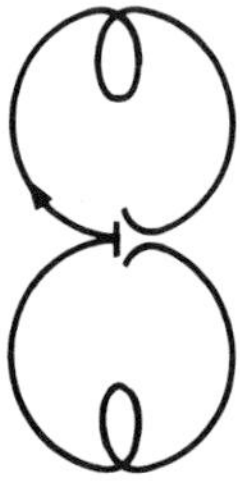

14

Loop

14.	RfoLPfo–LfoLPfo	3
15.	RfiLPfi–LfiLPfi	3
16.	RboLPbo–LboPbo	4
17.	RbiLPbi–LbiLPbi	4

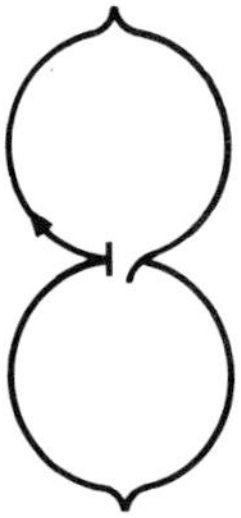

18a

Bracket

18a.	RfoBbi–LbiBfo	4
a.	LfoBbi–RbiBfo	4
19a.	RfiBbo–LboBfi	4
b.	LfiBbo–RboBfi	4

20a

Rocker

20a.	RfoRkbo–LboRKfo	5
b.	LfoRKbo–RboRKfo	5
21a.	RfiRKbi–LbiRKfi	5
b.	LfiRKbi–RbiRKfi	5

22a

Counter

22a. RfoCbo–LboCfo	4
b. LfoCbo–RboCfo	4
23a. RfiCbi–LbiCfi	4
b. LfiCbi–RbiCfi	4

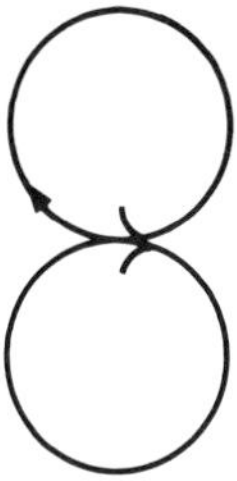

24a

One foot eight

24a. Rfoi–Lfio	3
b. Lfoi–Rfio	3
25a. Rboi–Lbio	4
b. Lboi–Rbio	4

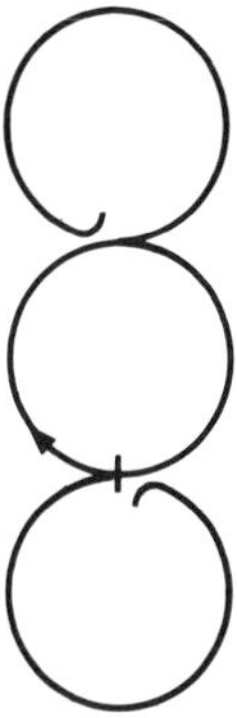

26a

Change three

26a. RfoiTo–LboiTfo	3
b. LfoiTbo–RboiTfo	3
27a. RfioTbi–LbioTfi	3
b. LfioTbi–RbioTfl	3

51

28a

Change – double three

28a.	RfoiTboTfi–LfioTbiTfo	3
b.	LfoiTboTfi–RfioTbiTfo	3
29a.	RboiTfoTbi–LbioTfiTbo	4
b.	LboiTfoTbi–RbioTfiTbo	4

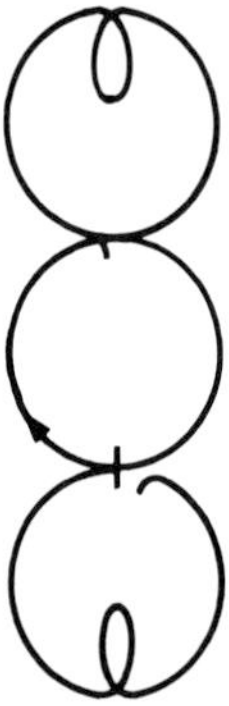

30a

Change – loop

30a.	RfoiLPfi–LfioLPfo	4
b.	LfoiLPfi–RfioLPfo	4
31a.	RboiLPbi–LbioLPbo	6
b.	LboiLPbi–RbioLPbo	6

32a

Change – bracket

32a.	RfoiBbo–LboBfo	5
b.	LfoiBbo–RboiBfo	5
33a.	RfioBbi–LbioBfi	5
b.	LfioBbi–RbioBfi	5

34a

Paragraph three
(three – change – three)

34a. RfoTbioTfi–LfiTboiTfo	4
b. LfoTbioTfi–RfiTboiTfo	4
35a. RboTfioTbi–LbiTfoiTbo	4
b. LboTfioTbi–RbiTfoiTbo	4

Paragraph double three
(double three – change – double three)

36a. RfoTbiTfoiTboTfi–LfiTboTfioTbiTfo	5
b. LfoTbiTfoiTboTfi–RfiTboTfioTbitTfo	5
37a. RboTfiTboiTfoTbi–LbiTfoTbioTfiTbo	6
b. LboTfiTboiTfoTbi–RbiTfoTbioTfiTbo	6

Paragraph loop
(loop – change – loop)

38a. RfoLPfoiLPfi–LfiF'fioLPfo	6
b. LfoLPfoiLPfi–RfiLPfioLPfo	6
39a. RboLPboiLpbi–LbiLPbioPbo	6
b. LboLPboiLPBi–RbiLPbioLPbo	6

Paragraph bracket
(bracket – change – bracket)

40a. RfoRbioBfi–LfiBbboiBfo	6
b. LfoBbbioBfi–RfiBbboiBfo	6
41a. RboBfioBbi–LbiBfoiBbo	6
b. LboBfioBbi–RbiBfoiBbo	6

36a

38a

40a

53

6 Early free skating

Free skating is, in a sense, the end product of figure skating. It is the more exciting, exhibitionist part of the sport – mainly comprising spins, jumps and linking steps – which the public admire so much, be it at the rink or on television. The technical foundation is laid by painstaking practice of at least the easiest of the school figures, from which good style can best emerge.

The meaning of the term, free skating, is that its performer is free to create an original programme, with minimal restriction on what is attempted, how it is performed or in what sequence. Free skating is what is seen in ice shows, skating exhibitions and the spectacular parts of figure-skating championships.

In shows and exhibitions, the emphasis is placed on what looks best and entertains most, adjusting the degree of difficulty to personal limitations and likely public appreciation. In competition, the choice of content is influenced by the need to include, in the most pleasing manner possible, as many different movements and the most difficult within one's capabilities within the time allocated.

The judges award two sets of marks to each competitor. The first is for technical merit, with difficulty of achievement and suitability of sequence particularly considered. The second is for artistic impression, when manner of presentation and interpretation to the music is specially noted.

Whether in competition or purely theatrical display, it is wise to remember that the free skating performer should *look* free. However tense one may feel, it is an art in itself to skate with apparent gay abandon, so a relaxed manner and confident appearance should be cultivated, not forgetting a smile to match.

Spirals

The most elementary ingredient and the first to learn in a free skating programme is the spiral. This is the name given to a forward or backward glide on one edge while holding the body in a posed position. An apt, self-explanatory

A typical spiral position with hands outstretched for effect and balance. The movement can be started with arms folded akin to sailor's hornpipe style, slowly opening them while gliding gracefully forward. The higher and straighter the free leg can be held and the more the free foot can be pointed, the more pleasing the spiral appears

description of a good spiral is a moving statue; the more graceful and classical poses that can be held during these glides, the more effective they will look.

They can depict various attitudes of feminine elegance or masculine strength; personal choice will vary according to ability and physical build.

The ideal to achieve is holding the position while gliding smoothly. Spirals come much more easily to the skater who has developed the ability to hold strong edges in figure practice. Learning a few variations of forward and backward spirals, then joining them together with suitable linking steps, provides the basis of a free skating performance to which turns, jumps and spins can be added and interwoven as progress develops.

Three turns

Before embarking on any jumps or spins, it is advisable properly to learn the simplest one-foot turn, the three turn – appropriately named because when performing it the skater traces an elongated numeral three on the ice. Turning the skater from forward to backward movement on one foot, this is the basis of the waltz in ice dancing and, though simple, must be learned correctly – and therefore not skimped in the early stages – because faults otherwise can easily develop and cause subsequent time-consuming problems, retarding satisfactory progress.

For the outside forward three, the skater turns from an outside forward edge to an inside backward edge, rotating in the direction of travel. Start in T-position, with right foot leading, left arm and shoulder forward, right arm back. Push off forward on a powerful leaning outer edge. The back should be straight and weight slightly to the rear of the blade's centre.

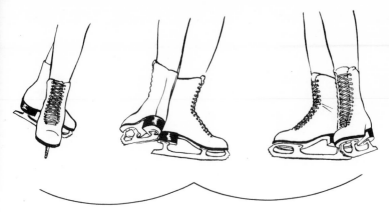

The three turn – positions of the feet. *Right:* the approach in T-position, right foot ahead on a strong-leaning forward inside edge, weight to the blade's rear. *Centre:* The weight has been transferred more to the ball of the foot, the back of the skate has lifted from the ice to swing a full 180 degrees. *Left:* the movement ends on the right back outside edge. *Below:* The elongated numeral traced on the ice by a three turn

Hold the skating hip well in and press the free hip and leg back. With posture erect, the shoulders can rotate against the hips until the shoulder line is almost square to the skating foot. In this position, the skate will almost feel like turning. The free left leg and foot are lowered until in a T-position behind the right skate. At the moment they brush lightly together, the weight should be transferred to the ball of the skating foot while increasing backward pressure on the right shoulder.

The body pivots while the rear of the skate lifts fractionally off the ice to swing a full 180 degrees before shifting to its inside back edge. Reverse the shoulder pressure and glide backwards, with free hip and shoulder pressed firmly back, weight on the ball of the foot, but with head still facing the direction of travel.

To retain correct balance, the head must remain erect throughout the turn. A reminder about what the skating

A dramatic spiral pose by Britain's Karena Richardson

knee should be doing: it is well bent for the initial push-off, gradually straightening as the moment of turn is approached, so that both knees are straight at the time of pivoting. The skating knee is then again bent at the moment of feeling the inside back edge.

All these directions for one apparently simple turn may make it seem at first frighteningly more complicated than it really is. The detail is merely stressed with perfection in mind, so that awkward habit-forming errors are minimized from the very beginning. Do it right from the outset and much time will be saved in the long run.

To recapitulate a few points – do not lean the body ahead of the skate, do not let the free leg swing out wide and do not let the free hip rotate forward. The turn is entered with the skating side leading; the turn is ended in backward direction with the non-skating side leading. All these words, yet the turn is effected as quickly as one can say 'lift round'. If a scrape is heard, the chances are that the rear half of the skate has not been sufficiently lifted the whole way round. Once the technicalities of the forward outside three on one foot have been grasped and practised, turning on the other foot is of course the logical sequel.

Three jumps

The art of jumping is dependent on the strength of spring and timing of take-off. Good height obviously is desirable, and early emphasis should be made on attaining this by consciously concentrating on projecting forward and well up before rotating. The rotation is started by pulling the arms inwards towards the body.

It is best to begin jumping the way round which comes more naturally. Most people, but not all, find it easier to turn anti-clockwise, taking off from the left foot and landing on the right. One can think of the other direction off the other foot at a much later stage.

The simplest jump to begin with is the three jump, alternatively termed the waltz jump. This entails a half-turn in mid-air, taking off from the forward-moving outside edge of one foot and landing on the backward-moving outside edge of the other.

If starting with the left foot, the skater first glides forward on the outside edge and begins to straighten the skating knee. Then, as – and at the very moment – the right leg passes (on its way out and in front of an arc) and the left knee is fully straightened, spring as high in the air as possible before rotating a half-turn in anti-clockwise direction.

1   2

The landing is made backwards on the back outside edge of the right blade, extending the free left leg behind. The knees *must* bend when landing. Try from the outset to avoid the temptation to concentrate so much on the rotation that height is neglected. One must not be content with a well-rotated jump only minimally above the ice. It suggests lack of confidence and looks 'wishy-washy'.

The three jump. 1: The skating knee begins to straighten when gliding forward on the left outside edge. 2: The beginning of the spring, with left knee fully straightened as the free right leg passes out and in front. 3: The mid-air anti-clockwise half-turn.
4: Landing on the right back outside edge, extending the free left leg behind. Note both knees bent and the non-skating side leading. As in all jumps the direction is optional.

3   4

This jump has been described as simple, but as with many elementary movements, there is infinite scope for perfection. The right timing, speed and height, which only practice can teach, can make the three jump a minor masterpiece of satisfying achievement.

A soft, smooth landing is the hallmark of a good jump. Endeavour to land on the toe of the blade edge while travelling backwards. This results in an agreeably quiet cushioning effect, so distinct from the harsh sound heard when landing incorrectly on the flat of the blade.

Two-footed spins

Having grasped the first essentials of the spiral, turn and jump, a summary of the rudiments of spinning will give a fuller elementary picture of the basic requirements in free skating. Most right-handed people revolve more naturally to the left and it is best to learn spinning as well as jumping in the direction which comes more easily, so those who find the reverse direction more natural will feel much more at home their way.

To perform the simplest two-footed upright spin – the best for learning the feel of revolving – the skater starts on a forward outside edge, as if to do a three turn, with arms held out to maintain balance. Allow the free leg to swing round and, as one turns into the inside back edge, the other foot is put down alongside the tracing foot, with toe turned slightly inwards. Draw the body upright.

A good spin is executed on one spot without any forward 'travel'. Any initial tendency to dizziness is countered by keeping the head erect and looking at eye level, not down

A characteristically dramatic spiral by Canadian Toller Cranston

David Santee, of the United States, in a forward 'moving statue' spiral

nor up, during the spin. Looking at the same fixed point each time round is as good a tip during skating rotation as when pivoting in ballet.

Any exaggerated rocking of the body, a common failing at first, could also cause dizziness and so must be quickly corrected. In short, a dizzy feeling when learning to spin will probably indicate an error of technique requiring adjustment. It is a teething discomfort which a normally healthy skater will soon overcome.

During rotation, keep the movement of head and body symmetrical, with shoulder line level. It is a good idea to end a spin with a jerk or toss of the head. This can be dramatically effective while, at the same time, clearing the vision. Pulling in the arms gradually to the body will gain momentum, but gradually is the operative word, especially while learning, or there will be a danger of acquiring too much speed too soon, which for the tyro could mean an unnecessary fall through loss of control.

7 Spinning without travel

Students of free skating who can perform all the elementary movements outlined in the previous chapter and seek seriously to broaden their repertoire will have reached a stage when lessons from a professional are strongly advisable if not essential. Before summarizing the descriptions and salient points of more advanced spins and jumps, a word about choosing a suitable rink tutor can be timely.

All ice rinks engaging the services of instructors for the general public should display on a board, by the desk or office where lessons are booked, a list of the names of resident coaches, their qualifications (i.e. proficiency tests passed) and fees per lesson. The fees normally vary in proportion to the qualifications.

Naturally, a championship-class skater requires the highest qualified coach available, but a skater who is only beginning to learn the basic technique of spinning and jumping will probably find a more junior teacher more appropriate because, apart from the fees being lower, such a professional will be more regularly accustomed to teaching near-beginners or moderate performers and thus more readily versed in the coaching techniques needed.

A highly qualified coach, on the other hand, is more used to teaching more advanced performers and may even have forgotten the best ritual way to coach at lower standards. To engage such a person is like getting the Queen's jockey to give a hacking lesson.

Dorothy Hamill, the 1976 US world champion, demonstrates her famous 'Hamill camel'

Sometimes the number of instructors at a rink can be counted on the fingers of one hand; sometimes there are more than twenty. After whittling the choice of coach to those specializing in a junior level of free skating (or in figures or ice dancing, according to one's need), it is wise to shop around, within the limits of the number available, to find somebody with a temperament most suited for striking a happy rapport – in other words, someone with whom a mutual respect and understanding can be achieved – and this depends on the personalities of both teacher and pupil.

As well as possessing the technical qualifications (amplified by membership of the national instructors' association), a really good instructor in any sport needs to be a good psychologist and have a calm temperament with infinite patience. Some pupils thrive more on kindliness than others, some require very firm discipline, some need humouring and some wish to be more constantly serious. Some take much longer to grasp things and should not be rushed. Sometimes, the more brilliant-minded can be surprisingly slower to learn something more practical than theoretical. These, if treated with appropriate patience, can become the most successful pupils in the long term.

So, hoping the right instructor has been found, let us proceed with a summary of details to remember about the most popular spins. A spin, by definition, comprises a series of complete rotations by the skater, either on the toe-picks or the flat of one or both blades, all while on one spot and ideally without 'travel'.

No motion of the body should be readily discernible during the rotations of a spin, other than the drawing in of the arms, after which the *gradual* lowering of the free foot down to beside the spinning ankle can increase momentum.

Even a simple single flat-foot spin on the flat of the blade, with balance over the ball of the foot, can look very elegant. A single toe-spin is similarly performed, except that the weight is on the toe-point. Small circles are scratched on the ice during its execution, which is why scratch spin is an alternative name.

The head must be held erect when beginning the spin. To gain momentum in one-foot spins, the arms and free leg are pulled in to the body gradually, an action which must not be hurried. When stopping, as the speed slackens take the free foot away from the skating knee and check the rotation by lightly touching the toe-rake on the ice while opening the arms out to the sides and checking the shoulder rotation.

Spinning should not be practised for too long at a time. Return to it every now and then after doing something different. At least seven full rotations of the body are required for a spin in proficiency tests. An erect posture and a straight knee of the skating leg are essential.

Two-foot and one-foot spins can be practised with several variations, on the flat of the blades or the toe-picks, on

The lay-back spin, a development of the conventional one-foot spin, bending backwards from the waist. The arms may be flung out wide and the free leg raised even higher to give extra dramatic appeal

either edge, forward or backward. A natural sequence is the head-back spin, with head held back as the term implies, or the lay-back spin, bending even further backwards with arms flung out wide for dramatic effect. Added theatrical appeal can be gained by variations of the free leg, especially if one's figure allows it to bend towards the head.

The parallel spin, alternatively named the camel spin, is performed with upper body and free leg parallel to the ice, in an extreme form of the arabesque in ballet with the back arched. This is more difficult than it looks because of the forward horizontal position of the head. Although normally performed with the skating knee straight, it is possible also to do it with a bent knee. Although called a camel, the less one simulates a humpy profile the more elegant it will look.

A further variation of the parallel spin is the grab-hold spin. To achieve this, after starting as an ordinary parallel spin the free leg is bent and the hand on the same side as the free leg grasps the rear of the skate when arm and leg are fully extended upwards.

More advanced still are change-foot spins, which, when well executed to a centre, lead to jumping from one spin to another.

The sit spin, created by the American, Jackson Haines, begins as an upright spin, the skater immediately afterwards sinking on the skating knee in a sitting posture, with the free leg extended in front. It is important to pull in the stomach and bend the torso forward during the lowering movement.

The free leg may be grasped by one hand or both and the head can be bowed exaggeratedly low for greater effect, but such embellishments should not be attempted before the basic sit spin can be properly executed. Another varia-

Dorothy Hamill in a graceful upright spin

tion is the broken-leg spin, in which the free leg – instead of being extended in front – is bent and held behind.

The sit spin position cannot be comfortably achieved without prior common-sense knee-bending exercises to flex muscles otherwise less frequently used. Even a normal knee-bend exercise at home to achieve a sit-over-the-feet position needs practice to become comfortable.

The most spectacular and impressive of all spins is the cross-foot, ideal to end a free skating programme because, when well performed and fast, it produces a fitting climax with a dramatic stop calling for instant applause. The cross-foot is performed on the forepart of the blades, with both feet turned in and touching, completely drawing in both

The sit-pin begins as an upright spin, the performer sinking on the skating knee with the free leg extended in front. The free leg can be grasped by one hand or both, and the spin is even more effective if the head can be bent lower

arms for maximum speed. Many believe that the toes should be exactly together, but greater speed is obtainable with the left toes about an inch from the tips of the right toes.

With perfect control and balance, it is possible to clasp the hands together as soon as they are close enough to do so. This creates a kind of leverage, and the arms can be

Two views of the cross-foot spin. Note both arms drawn in for speedy rotation, proximity of knees and both feet turned in and touching, with toe of left boot slightly behind the right toe

pulled in much more quickly. This has the effect of giving an extra burst of speed towards the end of the spin.

The star performer can add to the spectacle by moving one or both hands above the head after first gaining the necessary momentum. A good, really fast cross-foot spin is something to which the beginner may wistfully aspire, but which only the highly experienced skater can reasonably expect to achieve.

When individual spins and jumps (outlined in the next chapter) have been learned, the free skating repertoire eventually can be extended by combining jumps and spins – hence the flying sit spin and the flying camel.

In recent years, spinning unfortunately has been allowed to become, with notable exceptions, a relatively neglected art. The general downward trend appears to date from 1948, when the first jump to be achieved with three mid-air rotations, a triple loop, revolutionized the accent on athleticism in free skating, particularly at senior men's level.

The subsequent development of progressively higher and more difficult multiple jumps is, of course, commendable, but it should be remembered that variety is the spice of free skating. In the best interests of the sport it is to be hoped, therefore, that tomorrow's champions will come to merit being remembered as highly versatile performers and not merely good jumpers.

Dorothy Hamill performs an elegant forward spiral

8 Jumping with height

Apart from the desire to achieve as much height as possible, the essentials of jumping are a correct take-off and a clean landing. A faulty edge when approaching the take-off will cause an error of position almost certain to mar the whole jump. The landing must be made on the correct edge of one blade.

Landing precisely on a true edge gives the effect of a light-footed touch which is the hallmark of a good jumper, without which all effort to attain appreciable elevation is wasted. But it is a fact that the greater the height attained, the more easily a correct landing position can be controlled. The height, as instructors constantly stress, depends so much on flexibility of the strongly bending take-off knee. Delayed rotation is the modern emphasis – gain height first, then rotate coming down.

As has been said, everyone jumps the way round which comes more naturally, but those fortunate enough to possess ambilateral tendencies have an enviable advantage and can impress by showing the ability to jump in either direction and so display a greater element of variety in performance.

All skaters can execute some jumps better than others, each varying largely according to individual physique. Two of the most spectacular jumps, the spreadeagle jump and the split jump, are thus among the simplest for some (doing what comes naturally) and most difficult for others.

Starting from the simple spreadeagle position, with feet pointed in opposite directions, the spreadeagle jump can be performed on either the inside or outside edges, and is achieved by holding the original position until the last moment, when the heels are pulled closer together and a half-turn or full-turn is made in mid-air while maintaining the spread position.

Skating an even ordinary spreadeagle spiral is not easy for those with unsuitable build. It is something a slender, long-legged skater can usually do best and such skaters should cash in on this physical advantage. A long, well-controlled spreadeagle and a good spreadeagle jump are not all that common and are thus the more refreshing to see.

The same kind of tall and slim figure is also advantageous for the split jump, always attractive when done well. Obviously dependent on the ability to adopt a split position, the split jump starts from a back inner or outer edge, landing on a forward edge, and arms must spread out wide on either side, opening in time with the legs, to convey a mood of joyful exhilaration.

The always spectacular split jump, starting from a back inner or outer edge and landing on a forward edge. Note the arms should be opened in time and in line with the legs

Many leading skaters opt out of these two jumps for purely physical reasons, so those blessed with suitable attributes should seize the opportunity to do what others cannot.

The loop jump, which requires a full mid-air rotation, also provides the basis of several more advanced jumps. Taking-off from a back outside edge, the landing is made on the same edge of the blade. It is especially important to guard against rotating too early, in order to achieve maximum height.

The salchow jump, with an almost full mid-air turn, is performed after a forward outside three turn. Originated by the Swede, Ulrich Salchow, the only man to win ten world titles, it is begun on the middle of the blade from a back inside edge, and landed on the back outside edge of the other skate. Height is more important than distance covered. Perhaps the most effective alternative way of getting into a good take-off position is from an inside spreadeagle.

The lutz jump is a reverse-rotation leap, challenging because it is difficult to perform really well. The take-off is from a really fast back outside edge, with the skating knee bent as low as possible. The toe of the free foot is used as a lever to accomplish a full reverse (clockwise) mid-air turn, landing on the outer back edge of the opposite blade to that used in the take-off.

From the moment of take-off, a glance over the shoulder in the direction of the turn assists smoothness of rotation. Elegant style, close positioning of the airborne feet and graceful arm movements come only after diligent perseverance, which is why a well-performed lutz is particulariy satisfying.

Britain's Robin Cousins demonstrates the spreadeagle

The axel jump, named after its Norwegian creator, Axel Paulsen, requires extra rotation in the air – one and a half turns. The most important of the forward jumps, it can be very impressive when managed with good elevation.

Taking-off from a forward outside edge and landing on the back outside edge of the opposite skate, it is perhaps best described as a three jump combined with, and continued into, a loop jump.

The axel jump for the advanced free skater, taking off from a forward outside edge, with two one-and-a-half mid-air rotations before landing on the back outside edge of the opposite foot.

1 2 3

1: The take-off, with leading left shoulder indicating the direction of the jump, the landing of which should be made in the same line of travel. The free shoulder and hip are well back.

2: The thrust. After the take-off on a strong edge, the free right leg passes the skating leg and up (not around) to give maximum height and length to the jump.

3: The rotation. This is basically similar to that of a simple one-foot spin, with the right hip and shoulder turning against the left.

4: Hands and arms must not be raised above the shoulders.

5: After rising to the full peak of the jump, the free leg (prior to becoming the skating leg) is straightened with toe pointed down towards the ice.

6: The landing. The right skating knee is not bent until after landing. The free left leg must be held firm, with right shoulder now leading and left shoulder and hip well back

4

5

6

Power and a strong edge are essential, with knee bent strongly for the take-off. The legs should be kept fairly closely together while rotating, with arms near the body so that they can spread out at the moment of landing, thus checking any tendency to over-rotate and, at the same time, suggesting an air of confidence.

The reverse walley jump, originated by the American, Nathaniel Walley, starts from a back inside edge, landing on the back outside edge of the same blade. The turn is made in the direction against the natural turn of the edge.

The loop, salchow, lutz, axel and walley, and their respective variants (with or without toe-strike) form the basis of all the major jumps in free skating. Descriptions of take-off and landing edges are enumerated in the list at the end of this chapter. It may be helpful to emphasize at this point that perhaps the commonest colloquial terms used for important jumps are the cherry flip and flip. The cherry flip is the toe-loop jump and the flip is another name for the toe-salchow jump.

Multiple jumps are the same as those described, with extra mid-air rotations as their names imply (plus an extra half-turn in the case of axels). The commonest double jumps are the double salchow, double loop, double axel, double lutz, double flip and double cherry flip. All these can be achieved in triple form by top performers, but the triple axel is most difficult, very rare and, until March 1978, had not been accomplished in a championship. Even a quadruple loop jump is beginning to look within eventual capability. Like the now almost commonplace four-minute mile, once considered impossible, there seems little doubt that quadruple jumps will become a reality as training technique continues to improve, but it hardly need be underlined that multiple jumps are for the championship-class skater and single jumps must be mastered first.

It is reiterated that the technical details and hints set out in this volume are intended as complementary to the more comprehensive practical lessons available from qualified coaches, without whose guidance on the ice from time to time the reader is not recommended to attempt developing advanced ability in jumps or spins.

Jumps and their value

The following list describes which blade edges are used for take-offs and landings for each jump and the number of mid-air 360-degree revolutions each involves. The International Skating Union factor reflects the official recognition of difficulty. Thus, the higher the factor, the more marks a correctly performed jump merits in competition. Abbreviations used are:

f = forward   n = natural rotation
b = backward   r = reverse rotation
i = inside   TA = toe-assisted take-off
o = outside

Jump	Take-off	Landing	Revolutions	Direction of rotation	ISU factor
Axel Paulsen	fo	bo on opposite foot	$1\frac{1}{2}$	n	3
Double Axel Paulsen	fo	bo on opposite foot	$2\frac{1}{2}$	n	6
One foot Axel Paulsen	fo	bi on same foot	$1\frac{1}{2}$	n	3
Double one foot Axel Paulsen	fo	bi on same foot	$2\frac{1}{2}$	n	6
Inside Axel Paulsen	fi	bo on same foot	$1\frac{1}{2}$	n	3
Double inside Axel Paulsen	fi	bo on same foot	$2\frac{1}{2}$	n	7

Jump	Take-off	Landing	Revolutions	Direction of rotation	ISU factor
Triple inside Axel Paulsen	fi	bo on same foot	$3\frac{1}{2}$	n	10*
Loop	bo	bo on same foot	1	n	2
Double loop	bo	bo on same foot	2	n	5
Triple loop	bo	bo on same foot	3	n	8
Half loop	bo	bi on opposite foot	1	n	2
Double half loop	bo	bi on opposite foot	2	n	4
Toe loop	boTA	bo on same foot	1	n	2
Double toe loop	boTA	bo on same foot	2	n	4
Triple toe loop	boTA	bo on same foot	3	n	8
Lutz	boTA	bo on opposite foot	1	r	3
Double lutz	boTA	bo on opposite foot	2	r	6
Triple lutz	boTA	bo on opposite foot	3	r	8
One foot lutz	boTA	bi on same foot	1	r	3
Double one foot lutz	boTA	bi on same foot	2	r	6
Toeless lutz	bo	bo on opposite foot	1	r	3
Double toeless lutz	bo	bo on opposite foot	2	r	8
Salchow	bi	bo on opposite foot	1	n	2
Double salchow	bi	bo on opposite foot	2	n	4
Triple salchow	bi	bo on opposite foot	3	n	7
One foot salchow	bi	bi on same foot	1	n	2
Double one foot salchow	bi	bi on same foot	2	n	4
Toe salchow	biTA	bo on opposite foot	1	n	2
Double toe salchow	biTA	bo on opposite foot	2	n	5
Walley	bi	bo on same foot	1	r	3
Toe walley	biTA	bo on same foot	1	r	2
Double toe walley	biTA	bo on same foot	2	r	5

*The triple inside Axel Paulsen factor is estimated.

9 Putting it all together

Jumping, because of its spectacular appeal, naturally highlights a free skating programme and, because progressively higher and better jumps have been developed, these now dominate a performance to such a degree that the main criterion of a senior skater's prowess tends to centre on how many different triples can be achieved.

It is right that a champion should be an outstanding jumper of the class, but a skater who excels only in this aspect of the sport will not, or should not, become a champion if unable also to spin well and link major movements with intricate footwork to produce a versatile performance revealing all-round competence.

Free skating exhibitions – that is, non-competitive displays purely to entertain an audience – are usually in sufficient demand at every level of progress by rink managements, thus providing ample opportunity to prepare a suitable programme with subsequent competitions in mind.

The gala promoter may stipulate a time limit for an exhibition, but, if left to the skater's option, the right length of programme to plan is that which can be performed within one's known reasonable limits of stamina and ability.

Junior skaters with limited repertoire would be wise to concentrate the movements they can do best into a fairly brief programme rather than lengthen it without appreciably adding to the variety of contents. An unduly lengthy performance with a very limited number of quality contents, because more have not yet been learned, will make the fact more obvious than a shorter, more action-packed appearance which could leave the crowd more impressed. If onlookers thereby assume that the skater knows more than is exhibited, so much the better.

Short and sweet, keeping the action going, is preferable to long and tedious because of less frequent variations. Quality is more important than quantity during one's earliest displays.

Once having assembled – in mind or on paper, or both – a list of spins, jumps, spirals and linking steps known well enough to include in a programme, the choice of suitable music must be considered. The musically minded will derive considerable enjoyment from selecting the most appropriate piece, and experienced skaters with a keen musical ear and natural flair for interpretation will delight in arranging what suits them best.

The beginner is perhaps best advised to consult a music specialist at the rink. The person who operates the recording equipment is often ideal. One's instructor or a personal friend keen on music may help. Either way, the goal is to find a recording of mood and tempo to suit a programme planned with its most invigorating moves prudently spaced out to assist comfortable breathing and provide pleasing presentation.

The length of the recording – be it on disc or tape, according to rink facilities – must be timed to equal the intended length of the performance. Few young people today need much advice on how to manipulate tapes, which naturally eases the problem of merging a judicious selection of different musical pieces.

Two minutes is quite sufficient time for one's first exhibition. Both repertoire and stamina need to be built up before increasing much beyond that length.

East Germany's Anett Poetzsch leans well back during an inside spreadeagle

In senior championships, a main free skating performance lasts five minutes for men soloists, four for women and five for pairs. The duration is proportionately less for junior events. Normally a competitor is penalized by loss of marks if the performance either exceeds or falls short of the stipulated time by more than ten seconds – a reasonable safety margin allowing for human or mechanical error.

The art of satisfying an audience should never be underestimated. It is one thing to learn how to perform a number of different elements, but quite another to arrange the best manner of their presentation. The most suitable sequence by which to display a pleasing as well as technically fitting continuity must be carefully considered; also in what part of the rink each highlight should be performed to be seen to best advantage and show an overall well-balanced pattern. All this is a challenge to creative ability, so the development of a programme should be exciting and absorbing.

Whether it is an exhibition or competition, the free skating has either to please an audience or to satisfy judges, or both, so the best way to begin devising a programme is to plan a strong start and an impressive finish. Pull something out of the bag during the opening seconds which can best be done while still fresh and which will prompt onlookers to rub hands in gleeful anticipation. A slow, uninteresting opening is not recommended, so get in a good jump quickly. Not only can it be done best while fresh; its successful completion will boost confidence and make one *feel* fresher to do others.

Next, plan the most impressive finish possible to achieve when tiring. A spin is ideal, whether it be a simple upright spin within a moderate performer's capability or, for the more advanced, a fast cross-foot or flying sit spin. The former is a marvellous way to come to a quick halt and bow without anti-climactic travel.

Having determined how to begin and end, the middle of the programme can be devised so that the best variety of spins and jumps learned are spaced out fairly evenly and suitably linked as attractively as possible with steps and spirals.

After the opening 'audience-warmer', a spiral or two will help warm the muscles before embarking on other jumps or spins. How to space out the most strenuous contents must vary according to the individual's physique and stamina. Each skater, through practice, will learn the ideal point in the programme to ease up a little to regain breath and strength for something more rigorous to follow.

Even world champions have to 'freewheel' while getting back sufficient breath. It is up to each skater to camouflage these less vigorous moments with pleasingly artistic spirals and steps to retain interest and keep the programme alive.

Try to use every part of the rink so that the major moves are fairly evenly distributed. Avoid any habit of doing too many things in the same place. But, at the same time, plan the position of each move in such a way that there is minimal risk of touching the barrier. A skating exhibition or championship is not meant to reveal technical merit alone, but ability to present it artistically. That is why separate marks for each are awarded in competitions.

So the aim should be to use most parts of the rink with fairly consistent regularity while varying direction and tempo to sustain interest. The more spectacular elements, like a split jump, can be planned profitably for the centre of the rink. A series of loop or axel jumps help an impressive turn at one end. A sit spin will lose some of its effect if performed too near the barrier, where it could well be out of vision for part of the audience.

Some rinks, because of the way they are built or decorated, have their own little characteristics which may be different from others. Peculiarities of lighting may leave some odd shadowy spots. If possible, seek these out beforehand and adjust the pre-planned positions of important elements accordingly.

Having methodically devised a programme, with highlights suitably spaced out, positioned, attractively linked and timed to appropriate music, sheer repetition in practice should enable the skater to memorize the correct order so well that, on the day, it can be executed without hesitation.

When enough different moves have been learned, it is best to minimize repetition and concentrate on variety within one's ability. 'If in doubt, leave it out' is a good maxim during the early stages. Better to accomplish everything attempted than fail something not yet mastered.

While, admittedly, it is important to maintain full concentration on skating technique, an anxious or studious expression should be avoided as much as possible. A happy look is infectious and suggests confidence, so practise how to maintain a smile even when feeling blue. The psychological effect on crowd and judges usually reaps a worthwhile reward. The converse can apply when the skater looks sad, worried and ill-at-ease.

Although the use of an instructor is staunchly advocated with regard to technical skating progress, the preparation of a free skating programme is something which a skater with a creative mind and good musical sense should accept as a personal challenge. Though most coaches will advise about any points when asked, they know that the more original the creation is, the better. Here is the opportunity to express individual personality. That, after all, is the real purpose of free skating, to enable the skater to register self-expression rather than that of someone else. Seize every chance to introduce originality.

At senior championship level, it is true that there is a growing trend for stars to engage the services of professional choreographers. This emphasizes the importance now attached to artistic presentation, but, except for the élite few in the highest grade, it is surely more satisfying to 'do it oneself' as far as possible.

The ability to be original and, above all, as different as can be to anyone else, should be the goal to seek. Only thus can

A 'stag' jump by Canadian Kim Alletson

one hope to develop that special personality appeal, gimmick or charisma – call it what you will – that can put some skaters in that envied situation which commands added interest.

It is said that all really good artists in any branch of entertainment get nervous immediately before doing their thing. Sports personalities get stage fright just like actors. So expect to feel the collywobbles while waiting to go on. It is no bad sign and, magically, this tense feeling disappears once the performer confronts the audience and begins.

Those awkward prior moments of apprehension can be eased by concentrating on keeping the body warm and well wrapped until the last moment. Keep the legs active so that the muscles do not get cold. Many a tendon has been pulled through starting a rigorous exercise when too cold.

Never skate on an empty stomach. A light snack a couple of hours before going on the ice is ideal. Nearer zero hour, just before skating, it is a good idea to moisten the throat, and at major championships fresh orange slices are often made readily available to competitors for the purpose.

Another way to minimize nerves is by reducing some of the causes. Minimize the number of things which could possibly go wrong and reap the satisfaction of feeling 'fire-proof'. Peace of mind is a splendid thing. Travel with as many spares as possible, to meet any eventuality – alternative clothing in case the first choice gets torn or damaged, spare boot laces, needle and cotton, a duplicate recording, even a screwdriver and spare skate screws.

Expense may preclude everyone possessing two sets of skates and boots, but such would be a wise investment for those of competition and exhibition standard – not only as a precaution against loss, but in order to have a handy alternative, properly 'broken-in' set when one is being repaired or re-ground. When one's car is in dock, another car can be hired – but the very thought of an experienced skater using unfamiliar hired boots and blades for a public performance is enough to invite apoplexy.

When performing on a strange rink, check the ice dimensions in advance. If it is smaller or larger than one's own, the programme may need to be adapted to suit. If wearing new attire for a special display, give it a thorough try-out before the big day. Any possible fault, of fitting, fastening or stitching, must be detected in time for adequate repair.

There are two vital tips, so easy to give but so difficult to put into effect, which should be constantly impressed on competitors. The first is never to allow disappointing marks, whatever the cause, upset what is to be done next. Fully concentrate always on the immediate requirement, blot out from the mind anything previous, and the overall result will be better.

Secondly, never visibly reflect disappointment, however justified, at any stage of the event. A skater who looks dejected can hardly inspire a hesitant judge, but a confident appearance may sway the balance. Maintaining an amiable look in public, while and after leaving the ice, will win the high respect which such self-control deserves.

Many of the foregoing hints and suggestions are further amplified in *Let's Go Skating*, which complements this book. In some instances, alternative ways of expressing the same facts may be found to register with greater clarity to the reader of both volumes.

10 Pair skating

Why are there markedly fewer pair skaters yet many more ice dancers in the world than was the case a couple of decades ago? Ice dancing, the newer development in its present-day form, as a sociable recreation provides for many an initial attraction to skating. It is natural that a proportion of those who at first take it up lightheartedly become sufficiently fascinated to graduate to championship level. Pair skating is not taken up so casually. It is more physically demanding and one usually becomes actively interested from the outset with competitions a goal in mind.

But the fact that there are relatively few pair skaters does mean that the opposition is numerically smaller and so, for those who persevere, the mathematical chances of gaining recognition are much greater than in solo figure skating or ice dancing.

Because one cannot seriously practise pair skating without a regular partner, the importance of choosing a suitable one cannot be overstressed. It is one thing for two people to be ideally matched in physique, technique and potential, but much effort can be partially wasted if the pair are not also compatible in character and temperament.

It is necessary for the two to be able to achieve a happy rapport both on and off the ice because, hopefully, they will find themselves training and generally associating together for years. When an instructor and parents consider the merits of teaming a couple of youngsters, such long-term considerations should be given painstaking care.

Alex Zaitsev and Irina Rodnina, record-breaking Soviet world
pair champions, display neat alignment of arms as they go into a
death spiral

Many a young duo has been inadvisedly teamed solely
on the strength of skating ability and potential, only to find
after months or years together – costly both in time and
money – that they constantly argue and cannot get on
amicably. In short, their incompatibility is realized expen-
sively late. Generally, fewer males than females are available
and the girl of a broken partnership may not easily find a
suitable second partner of comparable standard to that
which she has already attained.

Compatibility, then, is an all-important qualification for
ideal partners. The man, of course, should be the taller
of the two. A slight difference in height will lend a pleasing
appearance. A greater disparity, if less appealing visually,
may be balanced by less physical strain in lifts.

Whereas ice dancers are required to keep their performance in character of recognized dance movements and tempo, with most lifts and other physically demanding feats of strength virtually taboo, pair skaters are allowed considerable freedom to create a programme displaying wider degrees of athleticism.

The main official guideline for pair skating is that the two partners perform movements which give a homogeneous impression. Synchronization or, simply, togetherness are alternative descriptions, which all really means that each partner's respective movements should blend harmoniously, whether or not in physical contact.

It does not follow that both partners need always necessarily perform similar simultaneous movements. Sometimes, each may choose something different, but they must strive constantly for a sense of unison and harmonious composition in everything they do. Lifts, spins, jumps, spirals and all other free skating actions are permissible, including anything newly created, except for certain purely acrobatic feats.

Competitions comprise two sections, short and long free skating programmes, both to music chosen by each pair. For the former section, worth a quarter of the total marks, each pair is required, within a reasonable time not exceeding two minutes, to skate six specified elements with connecting steps.

The composition of the long free skating (five minutes for seniors; proportionately less for lower grades) is up to the skaters to create in their own way. General rules governing lifts require the jumper in a lift to be assisted by the partner so that one continuous ascending and descending movement is achieved. This obviously precludes demonstrating sheer feats of strength by holding a partner overhead for unlimited time.

Partners may give each other assistance in lifts only through hand-to-hand, hand-to-arm and hand-to-body grips and not by holding the legs. This sensibly eliminates dangerous feats more suitable for the circus. Another move not permitted in competition for reasons of safety is jumping by a partner towards the other.

Teamwork is the keynote throughout, whether in physical contact or apart. The latter is known as 'shadow skating', when both skaters perform with unity of movement while separated. Each partner's arm, hand and leg movements throughout should correspond as closely as possible.

A typical pair sit spin position. Note the man's firm two-handed hold round his partner's waist and the alignment of their free legs. The girl can raise both arms above her head for an attractive alternative pose

Top left: Randy Gardner and Tai Babilonia perform a neat, fast-moving lift

Top centre: Alex Zaitsev and Irina Rodnina demonstrate superb synchronization of movement on forward inside edges

Top right: Alex Zaitsev and Irina Rodnina show strength and balance in a precisely poised overhead lift

Below left: US pair champions Randy Gardner and Tai Babilonia show a firm waist hold and neatly matched free legs in a pair sit spin

Below: This rare form of changing grip during a death spiral by the former US pair champions, Johnny Johns and Melissa Militano, is as difficult as it looks

Because each must do basically the same, the performance needs to be kept broadly within the technical limitations of the weaker partner, though there is no reason why one of them should not perform, say, a triple jump, while the other does something less difficult yet still with harmonious action.

The art of synchronizing matching solo jumps or spins needs little elaboration beyond the fact that it is fundamentally duplicating in harmony what one learns as a soloist. A pair's major free skating programme largely comprises a judicious intermingling of shadow elements with the more specialized pair movements. Typical of the latter are the death spiral, overhead axel lift, split lutz lift, lasso lift, catch-waist camel spin, throw axel and twist lift. To learn these and other pair elements, the services of a coach specializing in this form of the sport are clearly essential.

The death spiral is a movement wherein the man swings his partner round at speed while retaining virtually the same pose, the girl appearing to risk 'death' by her repetitive proximity to the ice while revolving round her partner, sometimes allowing her hair to brush the ice in the process. There are several variations of edges, direction and one- or two-handed holds. Controlled wrist and arm strength are key factors.

In the axel lift, the girl is turned one and a half times completely over her partner's head. After holding hands on one side, she is supported in the lift by the man's hand under her armpit. The lift begins from the girl's outside forward edge and is completed on the outside back edge of her opposite skate. The man rotates beneath the girl throughout the movement.

To accomplish the split lutz lift, both partners start from a side-by-side position, travelling backwards. The girl is lifted from a back outside edge. During the lift, she assumes a split lutz position. At the conclusion of the lift, she is travelling on a back outside edge and her partner on a forward outside edge.

For the single lasso lift, from a side-by-side, hand-to-hand position, the girl is lifted overhead from a forward outside take-off, turning one and a half rotations with the man's arm stretched (as if to lasso a steer) and the girl's legs in split pose. The man remains forward, to complete a backward landing on the right outside edge.

The catch-waist camel (arabesque) spin is performed with the free legs pointing in opposite directions, the bodies close together and arms around each other's waist. The spin by each partner is executed on the flat of the blade while the torso and free leg are parallel to the ice, with the back arched.

The throw axel and twist lift are two of the most popular modern developments. The former, when the lifted partner is thrown through the air from the force of a single or

The ever-popular death spiral, this one on a back inside edge, with the girl's head just skimming the ice. Note the girl's free foot tucked neatly over her skating foot and the almost continuous straight line of the four arms. This difficult perfect position is an ideal for which to aim

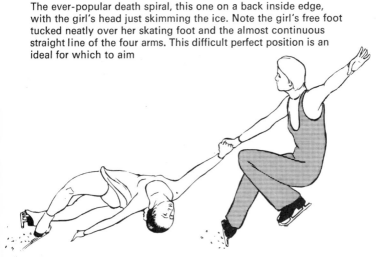

Above: Soviet pair skaters, Sergei Shakhrai and Marina Tcherkasova, whose unusual height discrepancy enabled them to perform the first quadruple twist lift

Left: East Germans, Rolf Osterreich and Romy Kermer, perform a delicate throw axel

double axel jump to a true landing, is so difficult that a fractured wrist has occasionally been the price of learning the correct timing.

Twist lifts involve one or more complete mid-air rotations by the girl while descending. Triple twist lifts are sometimes accomplished in major contests and one pair has even managed a quadruple, but only an abnormal difference in their heights and weights made this possible.

In both the short and long free skating sections of a pairs championship, judges award two sets of marks – the first for technical merit and the second for artistic presentation. Pair skating is a thrilling spectacle, demanding commendable skill, and surely merits increasing participation in the future.

11 Ice dancing

At many of the world's public recreational ice rinks, general skating sessions alternate with special periods for ice dancing. For the latter, only the more experienced skaters present can reasonably participate while the lesser-skilled majority watch, like wallflowers, in awe and admiration. The near-beginner cannot just have a go as at the local ballroom, but has to opt for *terra firma* because the firmer ground means less terror without proper tuition.

At this stage, the point is brought home forcibly that ice dancers need first to acquire a solid foundation of figure skating because most of the dance action on skates is based on the ability to hold firm edges, as figure practice can teach best. This is why ice dancing is so linked with figure skating, why an ice dance championship is so naturally a fourth event alongside figure championships for men, women and pairs.

It helps explain also why ice dancing is inevitably and rightly regarded as a sport. Before attaining Olympic status, there were serious suggestions that it be renamed rhythmic skating, a fair description, but the word dance is amply justified because this is skilful, artistic skating based on recognized dance patterns specially devised for performing on skates.

Soviet ice dancers, Andrei Minenkov and Irina Moiseeva evoke grace from toes to finger-tips

A good musical ear and rhythmic sense of timing are essential. To take up ice dancing without possessing these gifts is like learning to sing when tone-deaf. For those blessed with the necessary musical endowment, ice dancing has obvious advantages which make it a recreative sport ideal for family participation, be it brother partnering sister, father with daughter, uncle with niece or whoever.

There are no demands of strenuous athleticism as in the more complex lifts and spins in pair skating. For leisure enjoyment, it is therefore a reasonable activity to begin in adulthood, though for the ambitious competitors – as with all physical sporting pursuits – the younger one starts, the better.

The emphasis is more on good posture, which can be taught, and graceful alignment of partner's arm and free leg actions, the latter straight and with pointed toe more often than not. Because an elegant pose sometimes has to be held for four beats of music, correct positioning is vital to maintain the graceful appearance.

Although this chapter can only summarize the fundamentals, it would be wrong not to define a few of the most common terms unique to this branch of skating.

The *mohawk* is a half-turn, changing feet and direction on edges of similar character. Thus, skating feet are changed simultaneously with change of direction (forward to backward or vice versa), from an outside edge to a reverse outside edge or from an inside edge to a reverse inside edge.

The *choctaw* is a turn involving simultaneous change of direction and feet, but on edges of different character, e.g. from forward inside to backward outside.

The *twizzle* is a full 180 degrees rotation of the skating foot performed so rapidly that it is effected almost on one spot. The turn is made counterwise off an outside forward edge, with the free foot kept close beside the skating foot,

Grace personified by the Soviet six-times world ice dance
champions, Alex Gorshkov and Ludmila Pakhomova

ready to trace a forward outside edge when the turn is
completed.

The *chassé* is a sequence of three steps during which the
free foot becomes the skating foot without passing the
original skating foot, but is placed on the ice beside the
latter, which then leaves the ice slightly ahead of, or when
still behind, the new skating foot.

Senior competitions are divided into three sections. The
first comprises compulsory dances. In national or international championships there are three – any one of four
groups, drawn just prior to the event. These groups are:

Group 1: Viennese waltz, yankee polka, blues.
Group 2: Westminster waltz, paso doble, rhumba.
Group 3: Starlight waltz, kilian, tango romantica.
Group 4: Ravensburger waltz, quickstep, Argentine tango.

Other internationally recognized dances are the European waltz, fourteenstep, foxtrot, rocker foxtrot, American waltz and tango. Simpler dances are added to the selection for more junior events. Each compulsory dance must be executed in strict time to the music (prescribed for, and not chosen by, the competitors). The movements must be co-ordinated with the rhythm of the music so that all strokes are completed without break in continuity. The skating movements should express the character of the dances.

Provided that there is conformity with the basic requirements, some latitude in movement is permitted to enable couples to perform the dances with individual expression. Footwork must be neat and definite edges must be skated. Obvious double tracking must be avoided. On chassés and runs, the feet should be lifted as little from the ice as is consistent with taking a clean stroke.

The steps of the dances must be skated in accordance with the regulations for patterns, obtainable from national skating association offices. The couple should skate close together, with movements in unison and without apparent effort. The hold should be firm and the fingers neither spread nor clenched. In general, carriage should be upright but not stiff, with the head erect. All actions should be easy and flowing, with the direct object of assisting the movement. Speed should not be gained at the expense of good style. The knee of the skating leg should be flexible with a rhythmic rise and fall. The free leg should be turned outwards with the knee only slightly bent.

The second competition section consists of an original set pattern dance in prescribed rhythm, e.g. waltz, tango,

A permissible momentary lift by Soviet ice dancers, Gennadi Karponosov and Natalia Linichuk

Personality plus by Hungary's best-ever ice dancers, Andras
Sallay and Krisztina Regoeczy

samba, march, foxtrot, blues, rhumba or polka. The rhythm for all competitions in any one season is normally announced well before the start of each season in order to give participants adequate time for preparation.

The pattern of a dance is the design of the dance on the ice. A set pattern dance is one which lends itself easily to being so placed that certain steps are always taken at specific places on the ice surface.

Thus, the original set pattern dance must not be a free dance. Unlike the compulsory dances, each couple must choose their own music, tempo and composition. Only music with constant and regular tempo may be used. The dance must be composed of repetitive sequences consisting of either one half circuit or one complete circuit of the ice surface. Reverse direction is permitted provided it is maintained.

The dance sequence must not cross the long axis of the ice surface except at the ends. The choice of steps, connecting steps, turns and rotations is free, provided they conform to ISU rules. This does not exhaust all the possibilities of steps, turns and rotations. Any are permissible provided they are not toe steps and that at least one skate of each skater remains on the ice at all times throughout the dance.

The partners must not separate except to change dance hold, and this must not exceed the duration of one measure of music. There are no restrictions on dance holds, arm movements or handclaps which are interpretative of the music.

The third and final section of an ice dance contest is called the free dance. This, in contrast to compulsory dances, has no required sequence of steps. The free dance must consist of non-repetitive combinations of new or known dance movements composed into a programme which displays the personal ideas of the dancers in concept and in arrangement.

The free dance must be constructed so that the element of competitive dancing is predominant, and so that the free dance shall not have the character of a pair free skating programme. In the free dance, the competitors' general knowledge and ability in dancing, as well as the originality and concept of their ideas, are evaluated.

The duration of a free dance programme is four minutes for seniors and three for juniors. Each couple chooses its own music and this may vary in tempo from slow to fast or vice versa within the limit of three such changes.

To understand the limitations imposed by free dance regulations is to appreciate the differences from pair skating. Feats of strength and skating skill which do not form part of the dance sequence, but which are inserted to show physical prowess, are counted against the competitors using them.

Certain free skating movements, such as turns, arabesques, pivots, temporary separation of the partners, jumps, lifting of the lady, etc. are permitted with clearly defined limitations. Except for the purpose of changes of holds or position, only five separations of partners are permitted, each of not longer than five seconds' duration and at no more than two arm-lengths apart.

The combined total of arabesques and pivots must not exceed five. Pirouettes must not exceed five. Skating on toe-picks must not be excessive. Short jerky movements are acceptable only when they emphasize the character of the music.

Five small dance lifts are permitted in which the man must not raise his hands higher than his waistline. These lifts must not exceed one and a half revolutions. Five small low dance jumps are allowed for the purpose of changing the foot or direction of one of the partners, provided that they do not exceed one half of a revolution and that they are executed in dance position or at not more than two

112

The conventional waltz hold. Note the lady's right arm and man's left extended with elbows slightly dropped, also the lady's left elbow resting on the man's right. The man's right hand firmly holds his partner's left shoulder blade and her left elbow rests on his right elbow armlengths apart. Both partners must not jump at the same time.

It may be appreciated through these extracts from the regulations why a couple who may look the most spectacular may not necessarily merit the highest marks and that ignorance of these rules sometimes causes unwarranted public criticism of lower marks than expected for a 'flashy' performance.

The best known and most popular of the international dances is the *European waltz*. The earliest standardized dance, it was first performed about 1900 but its inventor is not known. Characterized by its cross rolls and drop threes, it is perhaps the easiest to learn fundamentally, but there is an initial tendency to hurry through anticipating the beat. Smooth, clean turns should be the aim, with threes (half-turns from one edge to the opposite edge on the same foot) turned between the partner's feet.

In the accepted waltz hold, the man's right hand should hold his partner firmly between the shoulder blades. The lady's left hand should rest equally firmly a little below her partner's right shoulder, her left elbow resting on his right elbow. The man's left arm and the lady's right arm should be extended and held sufficiently firmly to enable synchronized movement.

A couple should skate as closely together as possible in order to retain proper control. It is a common error, when learning, to hold one's partner at too much distance. The back should be arched and the chest thrown out. The body should be carried erect and over the employed skate, checking any inclination to bend forward at the waist.

The instructions for executing all the steps of every ice dance are fully set out and illustrated by diagrams in a standard ISU-approved booklet, obtainable from national skating associations.

British ice dancers Warren Maxwell and Janet Thompson in perfect unison with precise kilian hold

The *fourteenstep*, sometimes called swing fourteenstep, is a set pattern dance characterized by its march rhythm. It was originated in 1889 as a tenstep by an Austrian, Franz Schöller. Common early errors to master occur in the execution of mohawks, the man's tendency to double-track in backward movements and the lady's inclination to lean forward on backward chassés. To avoid inclination to walk or race rather than dance, it is necessary to cultivate soft knee bending and straightening with the rhythm of the music and so achieve an easy, graceful flow.

Another Austrian, Karl Schreiter, invented the lively *kilian* to march tempo in 1909. It is a test of close and accurate footwork, unison of rotation and control. Partners face in the same direction, lady at right of man, man's right shoulder behind lady's left. The lady's left arm is extended in front across the man's body to his left hand, while his right arm is behind her back, both hands clasped and resting at her waist over the hip bone.

The American waltz, not too commonly practised in Europe, is of uncertain origin, composed mainly of forward threes and six-count forward and backward rolls. The sequence of steps is simple, but it is difficult to control well the great amount of required rotation as a couple.

The *tango*, jointly created by Paul Kreckow and Trudi Harris in London in 1932, came as a welcome variation. Partners face in opposite directions, one skating forward while the other skates backward. Unlike the closed position, partners skate hip to hip.

The *foxtrot* was created in London in 1933 by Erik Van der Weyden and his wife, Eva Keats. With emphasis on soft knee actions and partners close together, this preferred pattern dance is seen at its best when performed with strong, well-curved edges. It expresses the syncopation of modern foxtrot music, skated not in the facing waltz position, but

116

The kilian posture, with partners facing the same direction, lady on man's right. Both right hands are clasped, resting over the lady's right hip bone. The lady's left arm extends in front across her partner's body to hold his left hand side by side, comparable to the 'conversation' position in the ballroom. Thus, with the man's right hip touching the lady's right, the man's right hand goes on his partner's right shoulder blade and the lady's left hand is placed on his shoulder. The man's left hand holds his partner's right hand, extended in front.

The popular *blues* to slow, smooth jazz rhythm was originated in London in 1934 by Robert Dench and Lesley Turner. Skated with bold edges, important here is mastery of the choctaw and there is challenging scope for effectively interpreting the slinky blues mood.

The Van der Weydens conceived two more dances in 1934 – the *rocker foxtrot*, which allows an attractive flowing movement, and the high-spirited *Viennese waltz*, danced at a good pace with strongly curved edges. The same couple in 1938 introduced the *Westminster waltz*, part of which is skated in kilian position, using the thumb pivot grip for the hands to facilitate the changes of sides by the partners. The lady's hands are held above the man's, with the thumbs extended downwards into the man's fists.

Three more dances were added in 1938 by Reg Wilkie and Daphne Wallis, the British champions from 1937 to 1946. They designed the *Argentine tango* – a difficult set pattern dance performed at accelerated speed; the relatively simple *quickstep*, characterized by its side-by-side swing choctaw; and the speedy, circular *paso doble*, which, as Wilkie himself observed, is 'quite an easy dance to do badly'. It involves unusual two-footed slide steps performed on the flat of both blades.

Yet another dance invented in London in 1938 was the somewhat unorthodox but impressive *rhumba*, devised by Walter Gregory. It is noted for a pronounced free foot side swing and smooth hip movements of the skating leg. It is skated throughout in kilian position.

The *starlight waltz*, yet another dance to be created in London, was invented in 1963 by Courtney Jones and Peri Horne. With the character and rhythm of the Viennese waltz, it is particularly pleasing to the eye and one of the easiest to perform.

The three newest dances to gain international championship status were all invented by couples who were themselves rival contestants. The *Yankee polka*, devised at Wilmington, Delaware, USA, in 1969 by the Americans James Sladky and Judy Schwomeyer, with their coach, Ron Ludington, is officially described as 'rather bouncy'. Partners need to remain close together to minimize the whipping action so prevalent when stepping quickly and turning rapidly round each other.

The *ravensburger waltz* was introduced at Krefeld, West Germany, in 1973 by the West German brother and sister, Erich and Angelika Buck. Another in the character of the Viennese waltz, with some steps in kilian hold and others reminiscent of the rocker foxtrot, this dance is elegantly adventurous.

The *tango romantica* was the 1974 combined product in Moscow of the Russians, Alexander Gorshkov and Ludmila Pakhomova, the first Olympic gold ice dance medallists, with their coach, Elena Tschaikowskaja. Romantically expressing the interpretative characteristics of the tango, it requires more than usual emphasis on deep edges.

12   Musical accompaniment

Because music is the food of free skating, read on. It is the food and the spice and the ingredients need to be carefully evaluated. A technically good free skating performance can fall flat without the choice of appropriate accompaniment and well timed interpretation.

It must never be forgotten that only half the marks for free skating are awarded purely for technical merit and that the other half are reserved for artistic presentation. Every phrase and bar of music should be considered so that major actions are timed precisely to a dramatic beat whenever possible. The music also should be descriptive of the mood of the programme envisaged.

The day has long since passed when anything but the waltz was considered incongruous to skating, though admittedly the waltz still remains ideal accompaniment for the beginner while learning the basic rhythmic strokes.

For first exhibitions or competitions, the choice of an 'undoctored' commercial recording suited to the skater's style and capability can be adequate, but the more developed competitive skater will be hard put to find an existing recording which by itself contains all the right climactic moments for jumps and spins ideally intermingled with quieter passages for spirals.

Eventually, passages from two or three records may need to be linked and this requires considerable forethought and skill. The music lover will relish this task, perhaps with the guiding advice of coach and whoever dominates the local rink's music scene, be it resident organist or music-room operator.

Skating is so much more than the pursuit of athletic ability on ice. The linking of it to music elevates a technically intricate sport more to the realm of a fine art. Abolish all thought of music as a mere background of agreeable sound because it must be so much more – the essence of a quality performance, to be heard as vividly as the action is seen.

First choosing the music and then adapting one's technical skating repertoire to it is far simpler than trying to fit a preconceived programme to a record. Orchestral music is recommended without vocal accompaniment. The latter, even when permissible, is seldom advantageous.

It is preferable if a suitable continuous passage of the required length can be found. If not, great care must be taken to merge two or more passages. A change of key or other lack of blend can easily mar. Connect tactfully, so that the merging may not offend admirers of the composer(s) concerned. In this context, it is more important to have a sympathetic understanding of music than to be a clever manipulator of tapes, so advice from a musical expert is strongly advised.

Tapes make merging so much easier than it used to be, but check the performing rights regulations and seek permission for public playing if and as necessary. Rink managements should be competent to answer any query about this.

Generally speaking, classical compositions are the safest bet for dramatic effect, but there is much to be said for the appeal of a popular new melody provided that it contains the required mood, right timed beats and tempo changes to suit the skater's repertoire. Something well known and of wide appeal can have a psychological advantage with audience and judges. A skater endeavouring to gain recognition can be handicapped with music which has not already done so.

The right mood of music, be it sad, humorous, vivacious, dignified or vigorous, will ease the task of miming gestures of arms, hands, fingers, head, face, neck, shoulders, waist, hips and knees. All require to be smoothly integrated. Remember that artistic impression means far more than how one skates: every movement of the body has its part to play.

The meticulous timing of interpretative skating to every musical bar and phrase means that the skater needs to know precisely the timing of the music ahead. This is why any human error of 'live' organ or orchestral accompaniment cannot be risked in competitions. The amount of necessary extra rehearsal time would be impracticable. Ideally, a skater in a really important contest would be best armed with duplicate discs and tapes of the same recording, to offset possible damage and any limitation of rink-playing facilities.

While infinite care clearly needs to be observed when selecting appropriate accompaniment for competitions, music for exhibitions is really another kettle of fish. The scope is enormous and there is ample opportunity to try anything out in a light-hearted atmosphere where marks are not at stake, mistakes are of less consequence and everyone tends to let their hair down. Exhibitions also can provide the chance to experiment with music under consideration for competition use.

The variety is boundless and all skaters of exhibition status find themselves listening to radio and television

Masculine elegance typical of John Curry, Britain's 1976 triple crown winner of the World, Olympic and European titles

music broadcasts with at least one ear cocked for suitability to skating.

When producer of a weekly skaters' programme on radio, I interviewed famous skaters before playing music with which they were associated. With few exceptions, they opted either for well-established classical compositions or more modern hits from stage and film musicals.

All who have watched skating stars in action, either at a rink or on the home screen, must appreciate the very wide range of music now being used, despite the fact that each linking step, every jump, spin or lift must be placed suitably to time. The music has to inspire and assist the skater's sense of interpretation and at the same time please the audience.

The *Light Cavalry* overture by Franz von Suppé and the stirring *Toreador March* from Bizet's *Carmen* perhaps have been the most used pieces by leading male free skaters because of the sense of masculine virility and superb percussion accompaniment for jumps. Canada's former world champion, Don Jackson, was particularly associated with the strident *Carmen* music.

In striking contrast, George Gershwin's gentler *Rhapsody in Blue* has appealed more to such famous women performers as Britain's Daphne Walker and the Czech, Hana Maskova.

Ernest Gold's theme from the film, *Exodus*, is especially suited for exhibition skating, opening and closing with drum-roll highlights ideal for impressive jumps and spins, punctuated with varied tempi conducive to graceful, ballet-type artistry.

Featured in touring Holiday on Ice productions, the

Former East German world champion Christine Errath adds helpful hands to the effect of an inside spreadeagle

finale of the renowned overture to Jacques Offenbach's *Orpheus in the Underworld* is the challengingly breathtaking can-can. Without, of course, properly attempting the too dangerous can-can on ice, the piece is highly descriptive and simply shouts for a concluding cross-foot spin.

Terry's theme from the film, *Limelight*, an example of Charles Chaplin's considerable ability as a composer, was used by the American, Gloria Nord, when she was chosen to skate in a Royal Variety Performance at the London Coliseum. It is perfectly suited for smooth-flowing spirals of balletic grace, with emphasis on hand and arm movements.

The Julius Fučik march, *Entry of the Gladiators*, may not be ideally suited for exhibition skating but some accept it as a challenge with crowd-pleasing results. The piece is widely associated with rink adherents as the signature tune of ice hockey teams.

The Skaters' Waltz is the best known standard music linked with the sport and of ideal rhythm for public rink sessions. It is probably the best liked of more than 150 waltzes composed by Peter Waldteufel.

All these pieces and more are featured on a stereo LP recently released on Decca SB710 in Britain and on the London label in Canada (SW 99561). It is called *Let's Go Skating*, similar to the title of my previous book, which is no coincidence because I devised the album and hope it will entertain readers usefully.

The magic atmosphere of the ice rink pervades throughout this special selection of music associated with skating and some of its star performers. Adapted to internationally recognized ice dancing tempo are the title piece, *Let's Go Skating*, a waltz by Reg Nichols and Harry Mann, and a three-tango medley comprising Victor Sylvester's *Golden Tango*, constantly played in ice dancing competitions, *Hernando's Hideaway* by Richard Adler and Jerry Ross, and Jacob Gade's *Jealousy*, which has been skated so well by the former Soviet world champions, Alexander Gorshkov and Ludmila Pakhomova.

Enterprising concessions and adaptations were made for this disc to suit skating requirements in a programme bound to appeal to lovers of the sport. Look for the spectacular colour sleeve picture of the former US world champion, Dorothy Hamill, photographed during her 'Hamill camel'.

Winter Sports is a sequel which I produced to consolidate a unique association with sports on ice and snow by the forty-two-piece concert band of the Royal Corps of Signals, under the baton of Lt Col. Keith Boulding. Their fourteen tracks, all on BBC Records in both stereo LP (REC 268) and cassette (ZCM 268) include the spirited and graceful *Les Patineurs*, which Giacomo Meyerbeer wrote for his opera, *La Prophète*, as a ballet for dancers pretending to skate.

March of the Swiss Alpine Club, with a style rather reminiscent of Glenn Miller, is another of several pieces in this album which should adapt ideally for skating exhibitions, the winter resort atmosphere being particularly relevant. The extra saxophones and clarinets shrewdly augment the brass, woodwind and percussion to produce a distinctive orchestral sound notably effective in a rink.

I have also devised a third LP played by the Signals band under Lt Col. Boulding's direction. Titled *Ice Time*, it consists entirely of music associated with the world's leading skaters, including *Farandole*, used by Charles Tickner, and *The Railway Children* film theme, now firmly linked with Robin Cousins. This is also a BBC Records release.

More specialized is the strict tempo music required by ice dancers and this is well provided for by a series of LP records played by the Max Greger orchestra with full ISU approval. Most rinks play these at ice dance sessions and copies are obtainable either through national skating associations or from Mr Beat Häsler, General Secretary, International Skating Union, 7270 Davos-Platz, Switzerland.

13 Speed skating

There are really two kinds of speed skating, outdoors and indoors. Unlike other sports on ice skates, racing in its best form requires more space than is practicable under cover. Oval circuits of 400 metres are the internationally accepted size for major events and, although there are now in the world more than a score of first-class electrically refrigerated tracks of that dimension, additional to the natural ice circuits in northern Europe and Canada, the majority are clustered in Holland, Norway, West Germany and Russia. There are three in the United States – at West Allis, Wisconsin; Keystone, Colorado; and Lake Placid, New York. Japan has one, at Sapporo, but there are none in Britain.

This means that a large proportion of potential leading speed skaters have to spend months abroad for training, involving considerable inconvenience and financial problems. Inevitably, the vast majority of speed skaters have to be content with pursuing their sport on the more limited ice areas at indoor rinks.

The status of indoor speed skating was elevated significantly in 1976 by the appointment of a new ISU technical committee for short-track racing ('short-track' referring to the indoor variety). The sequel in mind has been a belated institution of indoor world ice speed championships (outdoor titles date from 1893), to satisfy a demand from those nations with few or no outdoor circuits. The indoor sport must be regarded as second best because of the obvious space restrictions to technique and speed. But the newly gained status has given fresh heart to many indoor speedsters and the general standard of their skill, adapted to suit the smaller oval, should rise in consequence.

The speed skate is longer than that used for figures, usually between 30 and 45 cm (12 and 18 in.). The steel blade is as thin as a millimetre ($\frac{1}{32}$ in.) and is reinforced

A speed skater, clad in characteristic tights with woollen gloves and headgear, using full arm sweeps and cross-over leg action to corner at speed

E

above with steel tubing for strength and lightness. It is designed to travel straighter than the figure blade. Speed skates are not often permitted during general skating sessions at ice rinks, to discourage fast moving in the interests of safety. Their use is best restricted to recognized speed sessions and, in the main, during speed club activities.

The speed boot, made of thin leather, is more like a shoe in appearance because it has lower heel supports than that used for figures. It is also lighter in weight. Tights, sweater and, if outdoors, protective woollen headgear complete the attire.

Competitors normally race in pairs and in separate lanes, individual times deciding the final placings. To eliminate jostling, pack-style racing is no longer encouraged. The thinner air at high-altitude rinks is conducive to more favourable conditions, which is why most records are attained at venues providing this advantage.

The toe is pointed down more in sprints, to get extra ride out of the blade. Each gliding stroke begins on the outside edge of the blade and is rolled over to the inside edge as the stride ends. This accentuates a characteristic body-roll.

In distance races the blade strokes the ice at a ten-degree forward angle. The upper body relaxes above the skating leg. The straighter line one skates, the better. Strokes of 8 metres (25 ft) in length are achieved by top racers.

Over the longer distances, the skater sometimes races down the straight with both hands clasped behind his back, conserving energy while minimizing wind resistance. Sweeping arm actions assist speed and balance, particularly when cornering. The body, bent well forward from the waist, assumes a stance rather like the downhill skier's 'egg' position.

As an exciting, easy-to-follow spectacle, outdoor racing attracts very large crowds, particularly in Norway and

Holland. The indoor version is apt to be more confusing and generally less interesting to the casual onlooker. The smaller oval giving twelve to sixteen laps to the mile, racers naturally are more frequently lapped. With constant cornering and shorter straights, affording much less opportunity to gather speed, a different technique is necessarily developed which some find difficult to adapt successfully to that required on the large outdoor tracks.

World outdoor championship meetings are of two days' duration, comprising four events (500, 1500, 5000 and 10000 metres for men, 500, 1000, 1500 and 3000 metres for women), one title only being awarded to the best overall performance over the four distances, calculated on a points basis.

World sprint titles are decided at separate meetings (over 500 and 1000 metres for men and women). Titles for winners over each separate distance are recognized only in the Winter Olympics, when the men have a fifth event, 1000 metres.

Whether one begins speed skating indoors or out must depend on where one lives. Either way, if racing is the branch of skating which appeals most, it is best to join a speed club and benefit from the separate training sessions and specialized assistance thus available.

14   The art of winning

Skating as merely an occasional recreational exercise in itself can be pleasurably satisfying, healthful and socially rewarding. Many are content to limit their activities on ice to just such a modest degree of enjoyable leisure. This chapter is for those who seek appreciably more.

Once a skating bug has bitten hard, the type of bug must be recognized. Is the new addict to concentrate mainly on figures, dancing or racing? It is best to formulate some kind of general policy and plan a specific goal.

The first step towards reaching that goal is to join the relevant national association. In some nations, the same association governs all branches of the sport; in others, there are separate administrations for figures and speed, as detailed in an earlier chapter.

Training to pass proficiency tests should be the initial aim. These are graduated, starting with simple preliminary tests requiring very little experience and progressively scaled to earn bronze, silver and gold medals.

Certificates are awarded to all successful test candidates and one cannot enter a championship without holding the certificate which the relevant minimum standard of entry demands. As all tests and championships are organized by national associations, one cannot participate without being

A mood of gay abandon is conveyed by the expressive arm movements of the US world champion, Linda Fratianne

a member, so the need to join at the outset is obvious. The association supplies all details of test requirements and there is no point in duplicating such information here. More helpful will be tips and suggestions designed to increase the chances of winning.

A coach is an essential requirement to assist in a skater's preparation for tests. One simply cannot go it alone, but how much or little of a tutor's time is required depends on the individual. Some can absorb a lesson well enough to practise for long periods before obtaining further tuition; others need a trainer more constantly at hand. Either way, it is best not to allow enough time between lessons for faults to develop which might have been spotted sooner. Much time can be wasted by having to eradicate a technically bad habit that has gained a firm hold.

Judges are as capable of human error as anyone else. They are quickly blamed for harsh marking but seldom praised for leniency. In either event, they may miss something about which the skater is more conscious. So do not help them give lower marks than they might by looking dejected immediately after performing.

Always try to look confident and cheerful. This can have a bonus psychological effect. A judge hesitant about a possible error is more likely to give the benefit of any doubt to a skater whose very manner suggests having done well, even if the contrary be the case. A skater who looks proudly at a figure just traced is likely to be more respected by a judge than one who slinks away with a mournful tell-tale expression. Look challengingly at the figure before they mark it. Call it bluff or even mild gamesmanship, but it is a policy more likely to do good than harm.

The most vital advice is the easiest to give and the hardest to take. During a contest, try to avoid all concern about marks awarded. Concentrate solely on performing everything better than ever before. One's personal best in all circumstances is the sensible aim. The logic of this is irrefutable because the best possible marks should thus emerge.

So very many competitors have been shattered by just one set of marks lower than bargained for, whether blaming oneself or the judges. Brooding on such misfortune is fatal, playing on the nerves, upsetting the concentration and thus lowering the subsequent standard of performance. Each and every time something is required to be done, all resources must be centred on that one task to the exclusion of all else. A great maxim to have is: 'Concentrate on the job in hand and never let the mind wander.'

There was once a figure tracer of whom it was written: 'If a bomb had exploded at the other end of the rink, she would not have noticed – such was the depth of her concentration.' That particular skater completely disregarded whatever marks were awarded until after the contest was over. She was wise indeed. We all know that the golfer who broods on a fault at the last hole is more likely to lapse again at the next.

It should not be necessary to emphasize the merits of smart appearance. It reflects self-confidence and respect and this is infectious. A skater who is tattily attired, has failed to clean footwear or has unkempt hair is at a similar disadvantage to the one who looks miserable and omits to smile. Pride of appearance and an air of confidence can win over judges as well as the audience. Artistic presentation is an important part of the marking assessment and a skater of untidy appearance is also unlikely to be in constant demand for exhibitions.

Confidence is essential to success. It is the conviction of one's ability resulting from correct and careful preparation. Like pride of achievement, it is not to be confused with conceit. The latter is usually associated with a lofty attitude to others, wholly to be deplored. Any successful sportsman who remains unconceited is to be admired, but a need to believe in one's potential is vital if top honours are to be achieved. This is succinctly emphasized in a spurring adage displayed in this writer's office: 'He started to sing as he tackled the thing that couldn't be done, and he did it.'

Nearly every skater tends to emerge better either at figures or free skating, but all-round ability in both is the key to success in competition. Temperament plays an understandable role. The calm, studious skater with infinite patience and ability to concentrate is well suited to figures, whereas the impulsive, fiery and adventurous take more naturally to jumps and spins. Through its dual demands, the sport is therefore a good character builder, teaching the daring to be prudent and the careful to be venturesome.

The skater who shines in one department must work doubly hard on the weaker branch to avoid either being overtaken in the free or finding too big an initial leeway to make up. The moral is to devote due attention to both sections from the very beginning. Never neglect that which least appeals. It saves the later need to work desperately hard on one branch in order to catch up with a satisfactory standard previously achieved in the other.

We can all name skaters who have beaten the lot in figures, only to be humiliated in the free, and skaters who have dominated the jumping without ever a hope of winning the title. Take early counter-measures to avoid becoming one of these.

Whereas success in speed skating is determined by the clock, the final order in figure skating necessarily depends on the opinions of a panel of qualified judges. They are volunteers who love the sport enough to give much time to their task without financial reward. They are, in the main, honest and conscientious, though there are occasions when discrepancies occur through incompetence of one kind or another. The ISU strives towards perfection by suspending such offenders who do not satisfy the controlling referees.

If unfortunate enough to be the victim of a judge's error, however blatant, the skater should accept the decision just as the participant in any sport should abide by the ruling of appointed officials. The time and place for protest or complaint is not on the ice. If the error is palpable, others will be aware, and an ambitious skater cannot afford to be branded a bad loser in public.

All contestants must learn to be good losers, whatever the circumstances, to accept defeat gracefully and so live to fight another day. To be labelled a bad loser is to fall from grace with everyone. It is also important to be a charitable winner.

Part of the art of winning involves maintaining an ideal weight conducive to unimpeded performance. Metabolism – a word which, in layman's language, means the rate at which the body burns up food – is a factor of luck in any physical pursuit, dictating whether or not one has a weight problem to counter. Luck because, as many will have found to their cost, exercise alone does not always appreciably influence the situation. The contrary, in fact, is often the case with skaters.

Regular skaters with a tendency to put on weight often do so during the winter season and then shed surplus pounds during comparatively idle summer months. This is partly because exercise builds up muscles which weigh more as they develop. But, more important, it is mainly because exercise in the keen icy atmosphere sharpens the appetite more than when not skating.

Thus comes the greater temptation to eat all the mouth-watering things one should avoid when too plump. An overweight skater – that is, overweight because of surplus fat rather than muscle – is clearly at a disadvantage in the competitive field, particularly in those free skating movements demanding particular agility.

The point here is to be conscious of all this at the beginning of a promising career. If ambitious, but with a weight problem, eat sensibly from the outset by lowering the carbohydrate intake. This can be done by refusing sugar with beverages, cutting out sweets, cakes and puddings, and easing up on bread and potatoes. Prudent cutting down on the items mentioned will help sustain a trimmer figure.

To disregard this advice early and then, when obviously too buxom for successful skating, to embark on a crash slimming course, is most unadvisable. Drastic slimming in any case should never be undertaken without medical supervision. Losing too much weight over too short a period can be very injurious and can considerably sap the strength and stamina.

There are many lucky people whose metabolism is such that they can eat exactly what they like without it making the slightest difference to their weight or size. Those who are not in this enviable category can sometimes adjust their own metabolism by eating modestly and with fewer carbohydrates of the kind mentioned.

How to cut down on quantity of food? Strong willpower is only an initial and not a long-term need because it is a simple fact of life that the more one eats, the more the stomach muscles are extended and the hungrier one becomes. Conversely – and this is perhaps not too widely appreciated – the less one eats, the more the stomach muscles contract and the less hungry one feels. Thus it is within the power of most of us – other than those unfortunate enough to have some thyroid or other irregularity requiring specialized treatment – to adjust our bodies, whether or not we skate, to become as fit and active as our respective ideal weights allow.

What a lot of time and money can be wasted on a skater's long and arduous training if the question of ideal weight is disregarded when undue plumpness first becomes apparent.

Japanese champion Emi Watanabe wears a national-style costume to add exotic appeal to an exhibition.

If diligent application one day results in a skater being accepted as having a sporting chance to make the top grade, proportionately higher costs, e.g. in training, clothing and equipment, will be required. At this stage it is reasonable to seek some form of subsidy, either from the national association (sometimes able to recommend a public grant), an individual private sponsor or a commercial firm willing to support anyone who seems capable of gaining national sporting glory. If need be, and assuming that a justifiable case can be put, ask a sympathetic journalist or broadcaster to publicize the situation. In deserving cases, it is sometimes agreeably surprising to find how many people are willing to help if only the facts are made known to them at the time.

When in the championship class, one has to think in terms of extracting every possible extra ounce of know-how. Thus, one coach for figures, another for free skating and perhaps someone else for choreographic planning are thoughts worth considering. Another may well be the source of the extra money to pay for it all. Spoiling the ship for the sake of an extra ha'porth of tar is a major consideration if such an economy may mean the difference between winning a title and coming second.

What are the carrots, the real incentives for striving towards victory? For some, just the satisfaction of achievement. For others, much more. A title or medal can be a passport to starting at or near the top in a professional skating career, to say nothing of rewarding one's parents for money spent on earlier development.

Dedication and determination are the qualities, additional to talent, that are necessary to reach the top rung of the ladder. Given the unswerving resolve and willpower to succeed, attention to all the details which help the main skill can and must be given all along the route to victory.

15   Turning professional

Because so much pleasure, time and money can be devoted to developing a competent amateur skater, it is natural that a large percentage seek eventually to adapt the diligently merited knowledge and technique to a full-time professional career.

The two main outlets for this are coaching and performing in ice shows. In either case, one does not need to have reached the top grade to be able to gain lucrative employment. There is always a demand for instructors at junior level and for chorus skaters. If one has, for the former, a suitable temperament for teaching, or, for the latter, appropriate flair and physical appearance, it is possible to start a remunerative career after only a couple of years' skating experience.

As in all business, the higher the qualifications the better the opportunities. Whereas a skater beginning professionally as a very junior coach or an immature show recruit inevitably will take a long time to work up to a high position, the championship-class amateur may begin a paid career at or near the top.

There is no doubt that a title winner usually has an extra edge in bargaining power when negotiating a really good starting salary because the employer can cash in on the customer-winning advantages of publicizing the status.

Few readers will be unaware of the vast earning capacities which amateur titles stimulated for such as Sonja Henie,

Peggy Fleming, Karen Magnussen and John Curry, but they needed to be more than champions. Each also possessed a charisma through a special style and personality appeal which led to the really big money available only to an élite few.

But one does not need to be anything near so talented to be able to mould a happy, comfortable living from skating. Some have an instinctive ability for theatrical showmanship, while others – particularly those of calm temperament, more introvert and less inclined to travel – derive more satisfaction from teaching others. That is for the individual to decide.

There are plenty of opportunities for teaching at all levels in North America, Britain and western Europe. Vacancies are advertised in skating magazines as well as through that much-informed verbal rink 'grapevine' known well to every seasoned skater. A rink management or skating club director engages instructors of suitable number and qualification to cope with the likely demands of patrons. Most instructors operate in the self-employed category, their income mainly if not entirely deriving from their pupils' fees.

There is a steady demand for line skaters in ice shows. Three companies are especially well known for famous touring productions. Applicants for auditions should write a brief letter, summarizing skating experience, stating height and enclosing a full-length photograph. The addresses are:

Holiday on Ice: 2 Sheen Road, Richmond, Surrey, England, *or* 2 Pennsylvania Plaza, New York, NY 10001, USA.

Ice Capades: 6121 Santa Monica Blvd, Hollywood, California 90038, USA.

Ice Follies: Post & Steiner Streets, San Francisco, California 94115, USA.

These three are the longest established which offer all-year employment. There are also interesting three-month winter seasons at Wembley, London and other ice show promotions of varying size, any of which might offer worthwhile alternative attractions.

What are the necessary qualifications? For line work, which could soon lead to semi-principal parts if enough initiative is shown, one needs to have reasonably presentable appearance, a basic skating ability (jumping or spinning not essential), and of course, a natural leaning to showmanship and musical interpretation.

For girls, 1·68 metres (5 ft 6 in.) is an ideal height which would favour the chances, but a few inches less could still be acceptable if suited in other requirements. It is more difficult for boys to gain entry if under 1·72 metres (5 ft 8 in.).

It is usual, initially, to sign a two-year contract, which, assuming there is mutual satisfaction, can be renewed for an extended period. The basic pay can appreciably exceed what one would be likely to get in the average office job. Also, it can be almost tax-free while employed abroad.

Public transport costs, or the fare equivalent for car owners, are normally paid by the company. For those who like travel, the glamour of show business and a chance to see how the other half lives, it is certainly very tempting to be paid for doing what one probably most enjoys.

The more established amateur skater with a name and ability familiar to the general public – and therefore a calculable box-office attraction – should be particularly careful when signing a first show contract. If a strong enough skating personality, shop around to get the best offer. Play hard to get if past achievements have any bargaining power. Once having signed, it is not easy to win a pay increase quickly, so the higher the starting figure, the better.

143

Also, do not sign quietly without telling anyone. Get the maximum publicity possible. Contact the home town newspaper editor, who will almost certainly co-operate with a 'local skater makes good' story. If one is nationally known, contact any media representative who can give a boost, be it in newspaper, by radio or on television.

Always carry photographs, so that any feature writer who asks for one can be immediately satisfied. The small expense of photo-reproductions is in such cases a sound investment because, from this point on, a skater's professional career can be proportionate to the publicity gained. It costs good money to learn how to skate well, but, for those who so choose, a time comes to reap dividends.